Winning CHESS Openings

by
FRED REINFELD

Preface by AL HOROWITZ

COLLIER BOOKS
Macmillan Publishing Company
New York
COLLIER MACMILLAN PUBLISHERS
London

Macmillan Publishing Company
866 Third Avenue, New York, N.Y. 10022
Collier Macmillan Canada, Inc.

Winning Chess Openings was originally published in a
hardcover edition by Hanover House and is
reprinted by arrangement with the Fred Reinfeld Trust.

Library of Congress Catalog Card Number: 61-8902

ISBN 0-02-029760-2

10

FIRST   COLLIER   BOOKS   EDITION   1973

Macmillan books are available at special discounts for
bulk purchases for sales promotions, premiums, fund-
raising, or educational use. For details, contact:

Special Sales Director
Macmillan Publishing Company
866 Third Aevnue
New York, N.Y. 10022

Printed in the United States of America

CONTENTS

PREFACE

by Al Horowitz

One of the most profoundly disheartening of all intellectual experiences is the beginning chess player's first glance into *Modern Chess Openings*. Compared with *MCO* the *Principia Mathematica* seems eminently manageable, and a Sanskrit grammar even inviting. We shall never know just how many novice woodpushers have ventured unescorted to explore *MCO* and never emerged again, but the number must be considerable. We do know for sure that many players, who began with the intention to take up the game in earnest only to become discouraged by the sheer magnitude of the task before them, now confine their chessic activities to casual club play or to an occasional after-dinner game with their Uncle Harry or their nephew from Jersey City. And that's really too bad.

All this is not to denigrate *MCO*—far from it. It is an excellent and invaluable book, if used for the purpose for which it is intended: as a work of reference. It is the very thoroughness and comprehensiveness that make it so useful as a work of reference that make it appear so formidable, and it is growing more thorough and comprehensive with every new edition.

The first edition of *Modern Chess Openings*, sometimes called with varying degrees of reverence and irony "the chess player's Bible," appeared in 1911, the work of two otherwise obscure Englishmen named R. C. Griffith and J. H. White. Although it is all of 190 pages long, that now-rare book resembles more the traditionally termed slim volume of poetry than it does its more recent successors. The eleventh edition has recently appeared, edited by Walter Korn; it is 374 pages long and resembles any big fat book that one usually waits for to come out in paperback, and this despite the most strenuous efforts to weed out esoteric and outdated material. Remarkably, the format of all eleven editions is very much the same: brief introductions to each of the major openings followed by many many pages of chess moves, five long columns of them to each page, with voluminous notes and citations for each column.

Actually *MCO* is the most obvious, but far from the only, example of the more technical kind of chess-opening manual; it occupies its preeminent position only in the English-speaking world, and that only by waging an occasional victorious struggle against some upstart publication. There have been more books written about chess than all other intellectual games combined, and more books have been written about the chess openings than any other single aspect of the game. This preoccupation with the openings is by no means new; H. J. R. Murray in his *History of Chess* gives many pages of *Chaturanga* (Indian chess) opening analysis dating from the ninth century. Some of the earliest writings on the Western game, the undated Gottingen Manuscript and the *Repeticion de Amores e Art des Axedres* (1497), both by Lucena, are works on the openings. But we have come to witness in the past few years the gradual development of a new attitude toward the study of the openings, and an attention accorded to that study that sometimes transcends mere diligence and borders on fanaticism. This phenomenon is one of the most curious and the most interesting sidelights on modern chess, and to understand it some historical exploration is necessary.

By the time of the first international tournament, held in London in 1851, there had already appeared several books devoted entirely to the openings. The most ambitious of these was the *Handbuch des Schachspiels* (1843), the work of several young Berlin masters, the best known of whom was Paul Rudolf von Bilguer. Although Bilguer died before the book was published, it is traditionally referred to as his, and if many of the variations recommended in it look bizarre to a modern player its general layout is familiar enough; it is the genuine precursor of all subsequent opening compendia, including *MCO*. Nevertheless, no one thought to call it the "chess player's Bible"; many of the top players of the day knew it of course, and some even studied it with fervor, but other works were equally popular, and many of the best international players relied on no authorities at all, preferring either to do their own analyses or not troubling to analyze the openings at all, apart from their actual tournament play.

Despite the rather cavalier attitude toward opening theory that prevailed in some quarters during the mid-nineteenth century, it was at this time that the foundations of the modern game, in general, were laid, and this meant perforce that notions about the opening gradually changed. At this time two distinct chess "schools" could be discerned: a Romantic School, the spiritual heirs of the seventeenth-century Italians who had concentrated mostly on attacking play, and a contrasting school, to which no one has given a satisfactory name, that took as its model the great eighteenth-century French player François André Danican Philidor (1726–1795). Philidor had concentrated a great deal on evolving a theory of pawn play (the aphorism "The pawn is the soul of chess" is attributed to him), and his theories led in practice to slow and often ponderous positional maneuvering. In the clash of these two schools, each represented by some very talented players, modern opening theory was born.

Of course the greatest chess player of the nineteenth century, the American Paul Morphy (1837–1884), belonged to no school but his own and contributed more to the development of opening theory than anyone else. He himself never wrote a book, but exemplified in his play the basic rules underlying all sound opening strategy, and those games were subjected by others to the most careful scrutiny. He was apparently the first chess player in history to fully appreciate the necessity for the smooth and rapid development of the pieces. Because so much about the openings was *terra incognita* in his day, Morphy was able to find literally hundreds of important improvements in the practice of his contemporaries, and many of them simply substituted a scheme of straightforward development in place of some torturous and time-wasting maneuver.

Although Morphy unlike some of his contemporaries, was always intent on playing the best move at every turn from the first move on (as opposed to those who were happy just to shuffle their pieces out in the opening and then look round for a brilliant combination), he was never very interested in the opening play *per se*; that is, he never elevated it to the level of a separate study, nor was he interested in publishing opening analyses. Morphy was always concerned, first and foremost, in maintaining his status as a gentleman-amateur; to have devoted long hours to the study of the openings would have smacked far too much of professionalism.

Nor did the first generally recognized world champion William Steinitz (1836–1900), although an avowed professional, concentrate so much on opening theory as on a system of chess play that encompasses the whole of the game at once. Steinitz' doctrine exhorted players to accumulate small advantages that would develop into larger ones, and in turn into advantages of sufficient size to culminate in victory. In the context of this scheme he was far more impressed by relatively permanent advantages, such as material preponderance or superior pawn structure, than by relatively transient ones, such as more space or better development. Steinitz is the inventor of many opening lines still occasionally seen today, but in most if not all of them the side he favored secures some permanent advantage (usually material) in exchange for some extreme, although hopefully transient, disadvantage. Toward the end of his career Steinitz became an implacable opponent of all forms of gambit play. Many of his games show him snatching a pawn in the opening, even though doing so allows his opponent seemingly infinite short-range tactical opportunities, confident that he could gradually simplify the position and come down to a winning end game. Or else he would inflict on his opponent some weakening of his pawn structure, but in exchange concede so much space that he himself would spend the entire middle game with his pieces confined to the two back ranks, again with the expectation that his inherently sounder structure would tell in his favor in the end.

Steinitz' success with these strategical plans was based largely on his superb defensive ability, although it must be admitted that he occasionally took on defensive chores that proved too onerous even for him. To duplicate his success it is necessary to share in some measure in his defensive genius, and consequently, although his analyses and practice served to enrich opening theory, some of his own favorite ideas never became very popular.

Opening theory in the days of Steinitz' two immediate successors, Emanuel Lasker (1868–1941) and José Raoul Capablanca (1888–1942) was largely the province of lesser lights, because many of the top players, and especially the world champions, were downright indifferent to it. Lasker, although his pedagogical writings and game annotations unavoidably contain commentary on the openings, approached the openings rather casually: all he wanted for the middle game was a reasonably sound position (whether he stood a little the better or a little the worse hardly mattered) in which he could exercise to the full his vast combinative and imaginative powers. Often he was able to save even lost positions through his immense resourcefulness in the latter stages.

Capablanca, the child prodigy who learned the game at the age of four through watching his father play, and who claimed never to have opened a chess book until he was already of master strength, could of course hardly have been bothered to burn midnight oil over the openings. He writes of his victory against American champion Frank J. Marshall in a 1909 match (the final score was 8–1, with 14 draws) that:

> The most surprising feature of all was the fact that I played without ever having opened a book to study the openings; in fact, had Marshall played such things as Danish Gambits, Vienna openings, or the like (those openings that had been most extensively analysed at that time) the result might have been different. I certainly should have experienced more difficulty in obtaining such a result. I had only looked up an analysis of the Ruy Lopez by Lasker, on the P-KB4 defense, but the analysis was wrong, as it did not give the strongest continuation for Black. That, and whatever I know from experience or hearsay, was all my stock of knowledge for the match.

During Capablanca's reign as world champion (1921–1927) the so-called Hypermoderns (a group of younger players headed by Aron Nimzovitch and Richard Reti) brought about great changes in opening play, particularly in respect to the struggle for control of the center. Hitherto it was thought necessary to occupy the center with pawns at the earliest opportunity, but the Hypermoderns showed that it was also possible to control the central squares with pieces, and so defer the advance of the center pawns for a long time. Whole new opening systems grew up to embody this idea and its

negative corollary, that advanced central pawns are often
weak and may be made targets for attack. Lasker and Capablanca, who got most of their opening knowledge through
watching their fellow players in action, had little trouble in
adjusting their ideas about the game and taking what was
best in the new movement for their own use.

This seeming indifference to opening theory on the part of
the world champions naturally filtered down to lesser players,
and on the whole the first quarter of the present century
saw relatively little advance in that department of the game.
It was only with the defeat of Capablanca in 1927 by the
emigré Russian Aleksandr Aleksandrovich Alekhine (1892–
1946) that a passion for opening study became respectable.

Alekhine, in his quest for even the smallest advantage,
subjected the openings to a scrutiny never before heard of.
In the late twenties and early thirties none of his fellows
even remotely approached him in his encyclopedic knowledge
of the openings. The number of his contributions to theory
is enormous, and mostly reveal his extremely aggressive nature
and style; he is the discoverer of the modern strategical con-
cept of simultaneous play on both wings, and he focused
much of his attention on lines to assure Black ample, if risky,
counterplay.

The immediate impetus for Alekhine's opening-study program was his ambition to defeat Capablanca, but what ultimately made it possible was his passion for chess itself. American
grandmaster Reuben Fine gives us a vivid portrait of Alekhine
in his prime:

> The man loved chess, it was the breath of life to him. At the
> bridge table he would begin to talk about an obscure variation
> in the Scotch; on the train to Mexico he assiduously devoted
> four hours a day to the analysis of new lines; any game, played
> by anybody, anywhere, was good enough to sit him down to

evolve new ideas for hours on end. . . . He lived for chess, and chess alone.

Naturally the extent of Alekhine's passion for chess was as rare as his gift for it; although some tried to emulate him (like the Austrian player Ernst Grunfeld, who lived in a room stacked floor to ceiling with card indices containing thousands of entries on every opening), they were few and far between. The height of Alekhine's career, however, coincided with the growth of chess in the Soviet Union. There, where the government took the game under its auspices as part of the early Five Year Plans, with the intention to surpass the West in this as in other fields of endeavor, there grew up a group of subsidized professionals who could devote all their time to the development of chess theory. The Soviet players spent so much time and energy on the openings that the phrase "Russian Analysis" came eventually to be synonymous with any prepared line in the opening.

Apart from future world champion Mikhail Botvinnik (1911–   ), the development of the Soviet school was rather slow. It wasn't until 1945, when a team of Russians overwhelmingly defeated an American team in a famous Radio Match by superior preparation in the openings, that the Russian advantage in this phase of the game was apparent to the world. But although the Russians almost completely dominated the chess scene for the twenty years following the Radio Match, surprisingly little effort was made to copy their methods; some European professionals, mostly from the Eastern countries, became known as authorities on the openings, but in the West, and in America especially, the close study of the openings was often treated with mild contempt. When the twelve-year-old Bobby Fischer began to appear in the Manhattan Chess Club in New York with copies of Russian chess magazines in his back pocket, and quoted with seemingly total recall games played by foreign masters other club members had never even heard of, his knowledge evoked largely condemnation.

It is only in the past ten years or so, thanks largely to Fischer's successes, that the serious study of the openings began to proliferate in America. Some of Fischer's contemporaries, inspired by his phenomenal rise to fame, also took the plunge into the depths of Russian analysis, and even began to analyze for themselves. Books on the openings began to appear in English in ever-increasing numbers. Where before there was only *MCO* (which retained its central position on the scene only through increasingly frequent revisions), now there is a growing mountain of publications of every sort: other encyclopedic compendiums, books on individual opening systems, pamphlets on single opening variations, and of course a constant flow of articles in the monthly magazines. There are now far more games to analyze—more tournaments have been played in the past decade than in any twenty previous years—and far more players willing to do the analysis. The information explosion in the sphere of chess is as formidable as in any other field subject to similar social pressures.

In the light of all this, what is a poor beginner to do? Even if he has both the time and the inclination to plunge directly into the maelstrom, where exactly does he begin? And if he has neither the time nor the inclination, has chess indeed become too specialized for the likes of him?

Fortunately, the same grounding in fundamentals will provide both the serious student with a base from which to proceed to more advanced materials and the dilettante with most of what he needs to know to compete effectively against other casual players. Despite the floodtide of analysis that abounds in most books today it is still general principles that the begin-

ner needs to learn, and it is general principles that Fred
Reinfeld's *Winning Chess Openings* is written to provide. Here
the beginning student can learn, in a painless way, what the
openings are all about, what ideas underlie the different pawn
structures and patterns of development, and, equally important,
what to strive for in the middle games that arise in consequence
of the various openings. If the student masters the ideas behind the openings, rather then sets about to memorize specific
variations that he only halfway understands, he will not only
have more fun, but he will get better results, both immediately
and in the long run. If later in his chess career he takes up
serious tournament play, he will indeed have some memory
work to do, but it will be all the more efficacious if it is
grounded in a sound basic knowledge of general principles.
For someone who wants to learn chess just as a weekend
hobby, Reinfeld tells him what he *must* know—and if he
only masters what is contained in this book and never goes
beyond it, he will be able to hold his own in pretty advanced
company. And who knows—the lucid and witty exposition that
here, as always, is Fred Reinfeld's trademark, may inspire
him to take up the game far more seriously than he had at
first intended.

A DISCOURSE ON METHOD

Many a player has found to his keen disappointment that learning the fundamentals of chess is not enough to win games. "They laughed when I sat down to play, but they really guffawed when I made my moves."

What do we mean by the fundamentals? These take in the powers of the pieces; mating with minimum forces; making simple combinations; winning easy endgames—with a knowledge of these basic skills a player ought to be in business.

Yet this same player discovers when he starts practical play that he is usually defeated before he gets a chance to apply his knowledge of basic techniques.

And so he concludes from sad experience that he must have a good working knowledge of at least the most important openings.

He buys a "good" book on the openings—at least he thinks it must be good because it seems to have everything. He finds the book contains a thorough analysis, based on master play, of all recognized openings. This ought to be wonderful—but, to his bewilderment, he finds he is worse off than before.

Wandering through a maze of variations, he memorizes a few which particularly appeal to him. So back he goes to practical play. But what happens now?

His opponent, it appears, does not know the book, or, for some obscure but nonetheless annoying reason, very unobligingly does not play book moves! Again our mythical hero suffers the chagrin of quick defeat without a chance to demonstrate his newly acquired knowledge of the opening moves.

Often this type of player will improve—slowly and painfully, to be sure. But no matter what happens, his "knowledge" will always remain superficial and spotty. Come what may, he will never *understand* the whys and wherefores of the moves he makes.

MEMORIZING VS. COMPREHENSION

Ask the average player why the chessmaster plays so much better than he. You may be certain he will reply that the master knows the openings by heart—he plays from memory.

Can we really believe that the chessmaster's superiority is based on nothing more than memory? After all, when our typical amateur tried to improve his play by memorizing opening lines, he was unable to set up winning positions even against weak players! So we cannot escape this tried and true conclusion:

Learning is based on understanding, not on memorizing. That is the master's secret.

NORMAL FORMATIONS

What, after all, is the meaning of the statement that the master *understands* the openings? The meaning is this: the master knows the underlying *Normal Formation* of every opening he plays—and he knows it for *both sides*. He knows *where* every piece and Pawn should normally go—and he knows *why*. And—if we follow along this line of explanation—we must add that the master knows how to take advantage of any deviation from the *normal placement* of the forces.

Once you appreciate the importance of these patterns, you come to realize that prior knowledge of the *Normal Formations* is immensely useful. In fact, it is the necessary condition for becoming a good chessplayer. But the most exhaustive study of these same openings, if not accompanied by analysis of their respective *Normal Formations*, is a mere waste of time and may even be harmful.

What is an Opening?

Ordinarily when this question is raised, it becomes a merely academic problem of nomenclature. Should 1 P–QB4 be called the English Opening—or the Sicilian with a move in hand? But this kind of knowledge is not really knowledge. It is sheer pedantry.

From what has been said previously, you understand an opening only when you are familiar with its characteristic patterns.

Let's take some examples. Suppose we say to a master, "What's the difference between the Giuoco Pianissimo and the Colle System?" He will explain the difference by describing the normal patterns which apply to these openings. (See the following diagrams.)

Associate Moves with Ideas

What the amateur fails to realize is that all the opening sequences are attempts to lead to a certain ideal position. Consequently, it never occurs to him to associate these moves with a mental image of the desired pattern.

If he recognizes the opening visually at all, it is only when the moves are played over one by one. But set up a formation and then ask him to tell you what opening it represents, and he is at a loss.

That is why in our discussion of the ten opening lessons that make up the heart of this book, we will build up our analysis around the basic idea of the opening—the Normal Formation of each opening and the ways of exploiting deviations from the Normal Position.

Normal Formations

Before proceeding to the lessons proper, let's study two diagrams illustrating Normal Formations.

Normal Formation of the Giuoco Pianissimo

Diagram 1

BLACK

WHITE

Studying Diagram 1, we note first that each player moves his King Pawn to King 4 and his Queen Pawn to Queen 3. (This is the heart of the matter.)

Further, White's Knights go to King Bishop 3 and Queen Bishop 3. White's Bishops go to Queen Bishop 4 and King 3 (or perhaps King Knight 5). White's strategy may center on playing N–Q5 or P–Q4, or both.

Diagram 2 illustrates a sharply differentiated line of play:

Normal Formation of the Colle System

Diagram 2

BLACK

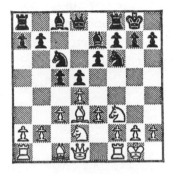

WHITE

White's Queen Pawn has gone to Queen 4, his King Pawn to K3 and his Queen Bishop Pawn to QB3. His Knights have played to King Bishop 3 and Queen 2. His Bishops are at Queen 3 and Queen Bishop 1.

What about Black? He has advanced Pawns to Queen Bishop 4, to Queen 4, and King 3. His Knights are on King Bishop 3 and Queen Bishop 3. His Bishops are at Queen Bishop 1 and King 2.

To the eye of the uninitiated player, there may not seem to be much difference between the White and Black setups. But the master sees meaningful differences.

White's King Bishop at Queen 3, for example, aims menacingly at Black's King-side. His opposite number, Black's King Bishop, on the other hand, is posted rather passively and threatens nothing.

In addition, White's Bishop at Q3 supports the powerful thrust P–K4. This will give White's game an aggressive character and will also open up a diagonal for the other White Bishop.

Black, on the other hand, is not in a position to play . . . P–K4. Consequently he will remain on the defensive and the development of his other Bishop will remain an irksome problem.

After reflecting on these differences in the Normal Formations, we are now ready to turn to the lessons on opening play. But even at this very early stage you can see how enlightening it is to be familiar with Normal Formations. Suddenly the chaos has lifted: you can plan; you can foresee; you have ideas; you can think about carrying them out.

WINNING CHESS OPENINGS

Lesson 1

RUY LOPEZ

(Morphy Defense: Strong-point Variation)

WHITE	BLACK
1 P–K4	P–K4
2 N–KB3	N–QB3
3 B–N5	. . .

Characteristic Situation of the Ruy Lopez

Diagram 1

BLACK

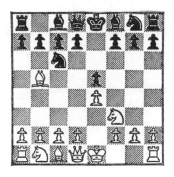

WHITE

This opening is among the oldest that have come down to us.
It is named after the Spanish bishop Ruy Lopez de Segura, who

is said to have played it in a tournament in Madrid in 1566! Yet the Ruy Lopez did not really achieve popular acceptance until about 1870.

Why this lag in achieving popularity? The point is this: the Ruy Lopez is a *positional* opening, involving long-range planning and intricate maneuvering and rearrangements of the forces. It appeals, above all, to the great masters of strategy. But this kind of play was frowned on in the nineteenth century—it was the era of slashing, smashing attacks. Sacrifices galore! was the reigning slogan.

How did the great masters gradually come around to position play and (consequently) to the Ruy Lopez?

The nature of position play

How does position play come into being? What makes it necessary?

The weaker your opponent, the more likely you are to be brilliant. He is bound to make mistakes, and this is the necessary condition leading to a brilliant refuting combination.

Furthermore, even if he doesn't blunder, you can still embark on risky play, serenely chancing the likelihood that he will fail to find the flaws—that he will miss his way in searching for the best defense.

Or take this possibility—you are playing against an opponent on your level of ability. Neither of you is too anxious about the outcome. In that case both of you are likely to play "brilliantly" (read "unsoundly"). The chances are that neither of you will try to defend yourself. Instead, each player will strive to strike back with an attack of his own. That is how chess was played, by and large, until far into the nineteenth century.

Then, about 1860 the prevailing tendency changed. This was partly due to the influence of the great Wilhelm Steinitz, the first

World Champion. It was also due to the introduction of regular tournaments and matches. To illustrate: the immortal Paul Morphy, the famous American master of the nineteenth century, played innumerable Evans Gambits and King's Gambits. But when we review the games of his formal matches, we find that he played the Evans Gambit exactly once in his matches—and his King's Gambits are almost as scanty.

Positional chess, then, is the kind of chess the masters play when they are playing for blood—for title, for money, for fame. For the most part, chess history since 1860 has illustrated the displacement of brilliant chess by positional chess.

Some of us may deplore the trend, and look back nostalgically to the good old days. But the player who wants to achieve winning results today will have to adapt himself to the prevailing style of our time.

What are the points that chiefly distinguish positional chess? Here are three aspects that need to be singled out:

1. Your opponent deserves respectful attention. You cannot beat him in 10 or 15 moves, because he will not make blunders bad enough to lose that quickly.

2. You cannot sacrifice pieces and Pawns merely because the likely sequel looks "promising." You must weigh the possibilities carefully, else you will give away more than the position justifies. In that case you will enable your opponent to escape with a black eye—and his loot.

3. Therefore you must play more patiently; build up your position, improve it in spots, watch alertly for a mistake by your opponent. If positional play is not his strong point, he will soon compromise his position, giving you a good opportunity to win incisively.

The normal course of the variation

WHITE	BLACK
1 P–K4	P–K4
2 N–KB3	N–QB3
3 B–N5	. . .

This move only threatens to threaten. At first sight it *seems* that White is threatening 4 BxN followed by 5 NxP winning a Pawn.

3 . . .   P–QR3

This is known as the Morphy Defense, after the great master who first gave it its vogue. It *seems* that Black is deliberately provoking his opponent to win a Pawn.

Position after 3 . . . *P–QR3*
Can White win a Pawn?

Diagram 2

BLACK

WHITE

No, White cannot win a Pawn; for after 4 BxN, QPxB; 5 NxP Black can regain his Pawn by 5 . . . Q–Q5 or 5 . . . Q–N4.

So White retreats and bides his time.

4   B–R4   N–B3

Black develops and counterattacks against White's King Pawn.

5   Castles   . . .

White does not fear 5 . . . NxP, for he has an aggressive re-
joinder in 6 P–Q4. In that case 6 . . . PxP would be very risky
because of 7 R–K1 with a dangerous pin on Black's pinned
Knight.

5   . . .   B–K2

Black closes the King file and thus threatens . . . NxP.

6   R–K1   . . .

White protects his King Pawn, which is now in need of support. And, as you will see later on, the Rook move makes room for
a later switch of White's Queen Knight to the King Bishop 1
square.

One more feature of the Rook move: by definitively guarding
his King Pawn, White now threatens to win a Pawn by BxN
followed by NxP.

6   . . .   P–QN4

Black heeds the storm signals: he drives off the menacing
Bishop, making BxN impossible and thus assuring the safety of
his King Pawn.

7   B–N3   P–Q3

This is necessary sooner or later to give really stable protection
to Black's King Pawn and also to open a diagonal for Black's
Queen Bishop. But at the same time Black has somewhat cramped
his game by closing the diagonal of his other Bishop.

White's prime idea in this opening begins to be clear: he aims
at *encirclement*, one of the great themes of positional play. If
White can attain his goals, he will constrict Black's position more
and more until finally Black is unable to resist when the final
break-through arrives.

Around the turn of the century White scored notable wins

Position after 7 . . . P–Q3
Black's position promises to be cramped

Diagram 3

BLACK

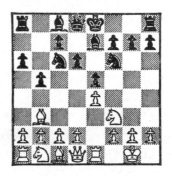

WHITE

with his encirclement strategy; but since then there has been a marked improvement in defensive technique and in the handling of cramped positions. The first Illustrative Game shows a satisfactory procedure for Black.

8   P–B3   . . .

White wants to form an imposing Pawn center with P–Q4. He avoids 8 P–Q4, NxQP; 9 NxN, PxN; 10 QxP?, P–B4; 11 Q moves, P–B5 and Black hops the unfortunate Bishop.

8   . . .   Castles

Black allows 9 P–Q4, which he reckons he can answer effectively with 9 . . . B–N5 pinning White's King Knight and thereby exerting indirect pressure on his Queen Pawn. White avoids this embarrassment with:

9   P–KR3   . . .

Ordinarily this is weakening or a waste of time or both; but in this case the advance of White's King Rook Pawn serves the useful purpose of eliminating . . . B–N5.

9 ...   N–QR4

The beginning of an interesting maneuver (see Black's next two moves) to give Black more terrain for his forces on the Queenside.

10   B–B2   ...

White's reluctance to let his Bishop be removed is understandable.

10 ...   P–B4

This is the key move made possible by Black's previous . . . N–QR4.

11   P–Q4   Q–B2

Now everything becomes clear. At Queen Bishop 2 the Queen gives Black's King Pawn the added protection it requires. Black is thus enabled to avoid exchanging Pawns in the center (which would free White's position appreciably). Thus Black's King Pawn remains the bulwark or "strong point" of Black's game.

Position after 11 . . . Q–B2
Characteristic situation in the Strong-point variation

Diagram 4

BLACK

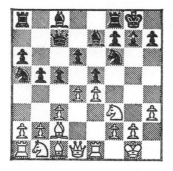

WHITE

What can we forecast about the future trend of the game? There are two main forks to be considered here, depending on whether White ultimately plays P–Q5 or PxP.

Characteristic position after P–Q5

Diagram 5a

BLACK

WHITE

This type of setup is shown in the first Illustrative Game. After P–Q5 the center is blocked and any future break-through, if and when it comes, will be on the wings. In both camps the King Bishop, hemmed in by his respective Pawns, usually plays a minor role. This can be understood by reference to the Normal Pawn Skeleton, as illustrated in Diagram 5b.

In Diagram 5b it is quite apparent that White's King Bishop is the prisoner of his Pawns on white squares, while Black's King Bishop is equally hemmed in by Black Pawns on black squares.

However, in the event that White exchanges Pawns early in the middle game—or late in the opening—we get a different type of position.

The Normal Pawn Skeleton after P–Q5

Diagram 5b

BLACK

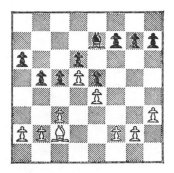

WHITE

Characteristic position after the Pawn exchange

Diagram 6a

BLACK

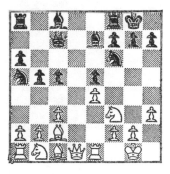

WHITE

Note how different this situation is from Diagram 5a. Here
the empty square Queen 5 (counting from White's side) is the

bone of contention. If White can plant a well-centralized Knight on this square, he will have a very strong—perhaps a winning—game. On the other hand, the presence of White and Black Rooks on the Queen file, with the resulting prospect of heavy exchanges, can do much to erode White's winning possibilities.

At all events, let's examine the Normal Pawn Skeleton after PxP for further clues:

Normal Pawn Skeleton after the Pawn exchange

Diagram 6b

BLACK

WHITE

Clearly the valuable center square Queen 5 beckons to a White Knight. Note, also, that both King Bishops have somewhat more scope here because of the removal of the Queen Pawn on both sides. The second Illustrative Game admirably sets forth the winning possibilities available to White.

White's Normal Formation

White's *King Rook Pawn* generally plays to King Rook 3. This prevents a pin by . . . B–KN5 and also prepares for P–KN4 in the variation resulting from White's P–Q5.

White's *King Knight Pawn,* as just indicated, generally goes to King Knight 4 in the P–Q5 variation, but stays at home in the alternative line of play starting with PxP. Why this distinction?

In positions where the Pawn center is blocked—as after P–Q5—there is little danger in a wing advance such as P–KN4. With the center shut tight, the opponent's mobility is not great enough for him to stamp the flank advance (P–KN4) as a weakness.

On the other hand, where the position in the center is fluid or open (as after PxP), a move like P–KN4 can have serious repercussions. For in an open position the opponent's mobile forces can reach the King-side very quickly, and White may discover that he has fatally compromised his castled position. These considerations explain, then, why P–KN4 is a poor move after PxP, when the center is fairly open; and why P–KN4 is a good move after P–Q5, when the center is blocked.

Note, by the way, that P–KN4 has several other uses. It tends to restrain Black's freeing attempt by way of . . . P–KB4. Also, in the event that White can post a Knight on the strong square King Bishop 5, it strengthens his setup enormously to be able to support the advanced Knight with P–KN4.

White's *King Bishop Pawn* generally remains at its original square. However, in the P–Q5 variation White may sometimes play P–KB3 to support his King Knight Pawn if he intends to play P–KR4 with a view to a Pawn-storming attack on the King-side.

Also, if White's Queen Pawn is still at Queen 4, White may play P–KB4, intensifying the pressure on Black's King Pawn. (Of course White has to remove his Knight from King Bishop 3 in order to be able to advance his King Bishop Pawn.)

Note, however, that if White has already advanced his Pawn to Queen 5, then P–KB4 is inferior; for in that case Black plays . . . KPxKBP and then plants a Knight at his King 4 which can never be driven away, as White has lost Pawn control of his King 5 square.

White's *King Pawn* plays to King 4 and generally remains there. In cases where Black has given up the center with . . . KPxQP, however, there are times when White can advance effectively with P–K5.

White's *Queen Pawn* advances to Queen 4. Sometimes it remains there, leaving the center in a fluid state and presenting Black with the opportunity of playing . . . QBPxQP with a view to opening the Queen Bishop file for his Queen and Rooks.

*The Normal Pawn Skeleton when White's Queen Pawn
remains at Queen 4*

Diagram 6c

BLACK

WHITE

Another possibility for White's Queen Pawn, as we have seen, is its advance to Queen 5. The intention is to block the center and cramp Black's game, so that it will become possible to attack him on either wing without his being able to counterattack in the center. (Some of this reasoning has already appeared in our discussion of White's King Knight Pawn.) Finally, the remaining alternative is for White's Queen Pawn to be exchanged for Black's King Pawn or Queen Bishop Pawn.

White's *Queen Bishop Pawn* is played to Queen Bishop 3 to prepare for the formation of a Pawn center with P–Q4.

White's *Queen Knight Pawn* remains on its original square as a rule.

White's *Queen Rook Pawn* often advances to Queen Rook 4 in order to engage Black's Queen Knight Pawn (which has advanced two squares). This advance may cause a weakness in Black's Queen-side formation, or it may result (after QRPxQNP) in White's monopolizing the Queen Rook file.

As for White's pieces:

White's *King Knight* goes to King Bishop 3 on the second move. The Knight usually stays on that square, except when it is shifted around as part of some long-range maneuvering scheme.

White's *Queen Knight*, on the other hand, characteristically indulges in intricate maneuvering in the development stage. It goes from Queen Knight 1 to Queen 2 to King Bishop 1 and then (after P–KN4) to King Knight 3. (This applies to the P–Q5 variation.) At King Knight 3 this Knight threatens to occupy the strong outpost King Bishop 5. Then, if Black plays . . . P–KN3 to stop the Knight invasion and to prepare for . . . P–KB4, the Knight at King Knight 3 has the function of restraining . . . P–KB4 or rendering it undesirable.

In the PxP variation, the evolution of the White Queen Knight's development would take this course: QN–Q2–KB1 and now N–K3 with a view to occupying Queen 5—or in some cases N–KB5.

White's *King Bishop* eventually lands at Queen Bishop 2 on completion of the triangular maneuver B–QN5–QR4–QB2. In the PxP variation this Bishop is fairly active. However, after the alternative P–Q5 the Bishop, as we know, is hemmed in by its own Pawns. This Bishop, by the way, is a bad piece to be left with in the ending, as it is blocked by its own Pawns on white squares.

White's *Queen Bishop* goes to King 3 or even (after Black's . . . P–KN3) to King Rook 6. In the latter case the Bishop keeps guard over Black's weakened black squares and takes part in the eventual King-side attack. The Queen Bishop is a good piece to be left with in an endgame, as it holds sway over the black squares unimpeded by the White Pawns on white squares.

White's *King Rook* goes to King 1 early in the opening. Later—in the P–Q5 variation—it may move over to King Knight 1, preparatory to White's building up a King-side attack after P–KN4. Or, on the other hand, the King Rook may shift over to the Queen Rook file if White has opened that file and wants to double Rooks on it. Still a further use for this Rook is on the King Bishop file in the event that White opens this line with P–KB4.

White's *Queen Rook* likewise has a host of possibilities. In the event that White opens the Queen Rook file by means of P–QR4, etc., his Queen Rook will stay on its home square. On the other hand, if White aims at King-side attack, he will play his Rook to the King Knight file or King Rook file.

White's *Queen* goes to the pivot squares Queen 2 or King 2. We use the term "pivot square" to indicate that at these posts the Queen is ready for action on either wing. Note, by the way, that it is important to get the Queen off the first rank so that the White Rooks can be in communication with each other.

White's *King*, after castling, will go to King Rook 2 as a rule to give the White Rooks maneuvering freedom on the King Knight file.

Black's Normal Formation

Black's *King Rook Pawn* remains at King Rook 2.

Black's *King Knight Pawn* remains on its original square in the PxP variation. However, in the P–Q5 variation, Black plays . . . P–KN3, creating a square at King Knight 2 for his King Knight or King Bishop.

Black's *King Bishop Pawn* remains at its original square in the PxP variation. However, after P–Q5 the ideal reaction for Black is . . . P–KB4. But this is easier said than done; for after White's P–KN4 and QN–Q2–B1–N3 and B–QB2 he has so many forces trained on the critical square that . . . P–KB4 is either impossible or, if possible, still disadvantageous. The general procedure is usually . . . P–KB3 (making room for Black pieces at Black's King Bishop 2) followed much later by . . . P–KB4 when circumstances are propitious. This procedure is shown in the first Illustrative Game.

Black's *King Pawn* plays to King 4 and remains there, unless Black has a chance to capture White's King Bishop Pawn (after P–KB4).

Black's *Queen Pawn* plays to Queen 3 and remains there in the P–Q5 variation. However, when White plays PxP, Black recaptures with his Queen Pawn.

Black's *Queen Bishop Pawn* plays to the Queen Bishop 4 square in order to give Black's Queen-side pieces more maneuvering space (Diagram 4). This Pawn has several possibilities in the subsequent play.

Note that in the PxP variation, the fact that the Black Queen Bishop Pawn has moved to Queen Bishop 4 is what makes it possible for White to dream of occupying Queen 5 (Diagram 6a).

If the center remains fluid (White Queen Pawn persisting at Queen 4), then Black has the possibility of playing . . . QBPxQP and thus opening the Queen Bishop file for his Queen and Rooks.

Finally, in the P–Q5 variation Black may push his Queen Bishop Pawn one square further to Queen Bishop 5. The object of this advance is to make room for the Black Knight at Queen Bishop 4—a fine post. (To arrive at this desirable square, the Knight will play to Queen Rook 4 to Queen Knight 2 and then to Queen Bishop 4.)

Black's *Queen Knight Pawn* goes to Queen Knight 4 in the opening. Sometimes Black can develop a Queen-side initiative by . . . P–QR4 and . . . P–N5, leading to the opening of the Queen Knight file.

Black's *Queen Rook Pawn* plays to Queen Rook 3 in the opening to drive back White's King Bishop. Later on, as just noted, Black may play . . . P–QR4 as a prelude to . . . P–QN5 with a Queen-side initiative.

As for Black's pieces:

Black's *King Knight* goes to King Bishop 3. Then, in the P–Q5 variation, the Knight often plays to King 1 and then King Knight 2 (after . . . P–KN3). Since this intricate maneuver may be hard to visualize, you can see it carried out in the first Illustrative Game. One virtue of having this Knight at King Knight 2 is that it supports a possible . . . P–KB4.

Black's *Queen Knight* plays to Queen Bishop 3 and then Queen Rook 4. In the P–Q5 variation this Knight goes to Queen 1 (after . . . N–QB3 or . . . N–QN2) and then to King Bishop 2 (after . . . P–KB3). This maneuver—likewise difficult to visualize—is also seen in the first Illustrative Game.

Black's *King Bishop* plays to King 2 and may later on continue with . . . B–KB1–KN2 (after . . . P–KN3) in the P–Q5 variation. This piece has little scope but it performs useful defensive functions. An important point: avoid being left with this Bishop in an endgame, as its maneuvering space will be virtually wiped out because of the Black Pawns on black squares.

Black's *Queen Bishop* plays to Queen 2 (in the P–Q5 variation) or may even remain on its original square. This Bishop supports Black's valuable objective: . . . P–KB4. In the PxP variation (Diagram 6a) this Bishop is more likely to go to King 3, to dispute control of the vital Queen 4 square. The Queen Bishop is a good piece to have for the ending. Not being impeded by Black Pawns, the Bishop has considerable mobility.

Black's *King Rook* generally remains on King Bishop 1 after castling. Here it supports the eventual . . . P–KB4 advance in the P–Q5 variation.

In the line of play in which White's Pawn remains at Queen 4 (Diagram 4), Black may play . . . QBPxQP, opening the Queen Bishop file. In that case his King Rook may swing over to Queen Bishop 1. In some cases Black may even double his Rooks on the Queen Bishop file.

Black's *Queen Rook* generally remains at its original square. Sometimes—as after White's P–QR4—Black may play this Rook to Queen Knight 1. Generally speaking, this Rook remains on the Queen's wing and is rarely used on the King-side.

Black's *Queen* plays to Queen Bishop 2 in the opening. Its later disposition will have to depend on the trend of the game. If the emphasis in the P–Q5 variation is on the Queen-side, the Queen may remain at Queen Bishop 2 or in some cases move to Queen Knight 2. If Black has to defend himself against a King-side attack, his Queen is likely to go to the support of the threatened sector.

Black's *King* will remain at King Knight 1 after castling. If the attack becomes too fierce, the King may shift to King Rook 1 or—in extreme cases—may even flee to the Queen-side.

ILLUSTRATIVE GAMES

GAME 1

(in which the P–Q5 variation is explored)

Baden–Baden, 1925

WHITE	BLACK
Sir G. A. Thomas	*A. Rubinstein*
1 P–K4	P–K4
2 N–KB3	N–QB3
3 B–N5	P–QR3
4 B–R4	N–B3
5 Castles	B–K2
6 R–K1	P–QN4
7 B–N3	P–Q3
8 P–B3	Castles
9 P–KR3	. . .

To prevent a pin on his King Knight, for as we know, 9 P–Q4, B–N5 gives Black troublesome pressure on White's center (specifically, White's Queen Pawn).

9 . . .	N–QR4
10 B–B2	P–B4
11 P–Q4	Q–B2

This gives us the situation of Diagram 4. Now White mobilizes his Queen Knight for the trek to King Knight 3.

12 QN–Q2	N–B3

(*See Diagram 7*)

By returning his Queen Knight to a position where it bears on the center, Black threatens to win a Pawn. Even 13 N–B1 does not adequately protect White's menaced Queen Pawn, for there follows 13 . . . BPxP; 14 PxP, PxP and White must not reply 15 NxP? because of 15 . . . NxN and Black wins a piece.

Position after 12 . . . N–B3
Black threatens to win a Pawn

Diagram 7

BLACK

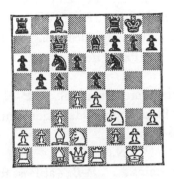

WHITE

13   P–Q5   . . .

This move has an immediate as well as long-term significance. It solves the problem of protecting White's Queen Pawn. But the remoter implication is that White wishes to undertake a King-side attack; hence he stabilizes the center. This leads to a very complex situation in which Black must play with exemplary coolness.

13   . . .   N–Q1

This Knight momentarily has no mobility, but he is on his way to King Bishop 2 (after Black has made room for the Knight).

14   N–B1   N–K1

This makes room for . . . P–B3, which in turn makes room for the other Knight.

15   P–QR4   . . .

He tries to divert Black's attention from the King-side. White's immediate threat is PxP winning a Pawn as Black's Queen Rook Pawn is pinned.

15 . . .   R–N1

This parries White's threat by getting the Rook off the Queen Rook file.

16 PxP   . . .

Giving White the open Queen Rook file, but the question is: can he control it indefinitely? Probably 16 P–B4 was more exact. Then if Black replies 16 . . . PxBP White replies 17 QN–Q2 followed by NxBP with a magnificent post for his Queen Knight. If Black tries 16 . . . NPxRP he is left with a weak Queen Rook Pawn.

Best for Black, therefore, seems 16 . . . P–N5. But in that case all counterplay for Black on the Queen-side is ruled out.

16 . . .   PxP

17 P–KN4   . . .

This advance restrains . . . P–B4—at least for the time being.

Position after 17 P–KN4
The following play centers around
Black's desire to play . . . P–B4.

Diagram 8

BLACK

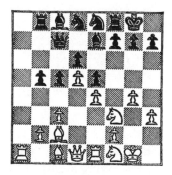

WHITE

                17 . . .   P–N3

This move supports an eventual . . . P–B4 and also makes
room for the Black Knight now at King 1.

                18 N–N3   . . .

White prevents . . . P–B4.

                18 . . .   N–KN2

Black strives for . . . P–B4.

                19 K–R1   . . .

Although the connection may not appear obvious, this is re-
lated to Black's striving for . . . P–B4. The point of the King
move is that it allows White to occupy the King Knight file if
need be.

   Here is a plausible possibility: 19 . . . P–B4; 20 NPxP, PxP;
21 PxP, NxP; 22 NxN, BxN; 23 BxB, RxB; 24 R–KN1ch,
K–R1; 25 N–Q4!, R–KB1 (if 25 . . . PxN; 26 Q–N4, wins because of White's mate threat coupled with the threat of QxR);

Position after 19 K–R1
Black makes haste slowly

Diagram 9

BLACK

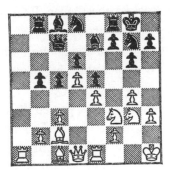

WHITE

26 Q–N4, B–B3; 27 B–R6, R–K1; 28 Q–B5 with a winning attack for White.

This variation is important as showing us how circumspect Black must be in achieving his intended goal . . . P–B4.

White's clearing of the King Knight file with the King move is commendable. Nevertheless 19 K–R1 is an inexactitude, and 19 K–R2 would have been more to the point. Why this is so, will become clear a little later on.

19 . . .   P–B3

We have just seen that 19 . . . P–B4 would be premature. Hence Black discreetly limits himself to advancing one square.

20 R–KN1   . . .

This definitely discourages . . . P–B4 because of the subtly masked action on the King Knight file—for example 20 . . . P–B4?; 21 NPxP, PxP; 22 PxP, BxP??; 23 NxB and Black is lost, as his Knight is pinned on the King Knight file.

20 . . .   N–B2

Note how carefully and solidly Black builds up his position on the King-side.

21 Q–B1   . . .

More usual is Q–K2 followed by B–K3 and the doubling of White's Rooks on the King Knight file. In this situation, however, that popular plan is of dubious value, as it would allow Black to return his Queen Rook to the Queen Rook file, with a certain amount of Queen-side counterplay.

Such a diversion would demand enough attention from White to put a crimp in his King-side attacking plans.

21 . . .   B–Q2

In contrast to White's hesitant procedure Black develops purposefully. His last move has established contact between his Rooks, so that he can now dispute control of the open Queen Rook file.

22 B–K3   R–R1!

Position after 22 . . . R–R1!
The position begins to favor Black

Diagram 10

BLACK

WHITE

Black's fight for control of the Queen Rook file is cleverly thought out. If White abandons the file he concedes Black an important strategical advantage. If on the other hand White tries to hold the file all the Rooks will be exchanged. Once this blood-letting has occurred, White's chances of attack have evaporated.

23	Q–N2	RxR
24	RxR	Q–N2

Foreshadowing Black's next move.

25	K–R2	. . .

Having lost the initiative, White is content to adopt a waiting policy.

25	. . .	R–R1
26	Q–B1	R–R3!

This maneuver gives Black control of the Queen Rook file.

27	N–Q2	Q–R1
28	RxR	QxR

29 N–N3 . . .

White is fully prepared for 29 . . . Q–R7, which he can answer with 30 Q–QR1 or Q–QN1. But Black is ready to shift to the other wing now.

29 . . . N–N4!

Position after 29 . . . N–N4!
Black seizes the initiative

Diagram 11

BLACK

WHITE

Black has taken advantage of the absence of White's King Knight to start a surprisingly effective attack on White's weak points on the King-side. White's King Rook Pawn is the main target, thanks to the threat of . . . P–R4!

It is not easy to find a satisfactory reply to the provocative Knight move. For example, if 30 P–R4?, N–B6ch; 31 K–R3, P–R4 and White's game is in ruins.

It is true that White can eliminate his immediate troubles with 30 BxN, but after 30 . . . PxB; 31 P–B3, P–B5; 32 N–Q2, P–R4! we find that Black is steadily gaining ground. Black has the

Bishop-pair—a real asset in this position—as well as strong play
on White's weakened black squares. In addition, White is left
with his inferior Bishop. The play might go 33 Q–K2, B–Q1!
followed by . . . B–N3! and the gradual build-up of irresistible
Black pressure.

30   K–N2   P–R4!

Obviously White cannot reply 31 PxP?? because of 31 . . .
BxPch winning the White Queen. Best was 31 P–B3.

31   P–R4   . . .

While White's impatience is understandable, this move has
the drawback of making White's position more vulnerable. Why
this is so is by no means obvious to an inexperienced player, and
it is therefore very instructive to follow the coming play.

31   . . .   N–B2
32   PxP   PxP
33   K–R2   Q–B1!

Position after 33 . . . Q–B1!
Black is at last preparing for . . . P–B4!

Diagram 12

BLACK

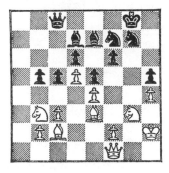

WHITE

All this time Black's Queen has been seemingly out of play, far from the main scene of action. Suddenly Black's counterplay is appreciably strengthened by the approaching . . . P–B4. Black's hitherto inactive King Bishop will come to life and the natural protection of White's Queen Pawn will disappear. Above all, White's Rook Pawn is not long for this world.

34   Q–N2   . . .

White threatens 35 NxRP and also prevents . . . P–B4. But Black puts an end to this by unpinning his pinned Knight.

34   . . .   K–B1
35   N–Q2   P–B4!

At last! To begin with, this move wins White's Rook Pawn.

36   PxP   . . .

More or less forced, as Black was threatening to win a piece with . . . P–B5.

36   . . .   BxRP

Now Black must win a Pawn, for example 37 Q–R3, BxNch; 38 PxB, BxP etc.

37   P–B6!   . . .

A good move which greatly increases Black's technical difficulties. The Pawn is untenable in any event. White therefore gives it up in such a way that he gets the initiative for a while and thus slows up Black's winning process.

37   . . .   BxP
38   Q–B3!   . . .

This seems to regain the Pawn.

(See Diagram 13)

How is Black to hold on to his Pawn? On 38 . . . B–K2; 39 B–N6 regains the Pawn at once. On 38 . . . Q–Q1; 39 NxRP is possible. And if 38 . . . K–K2; 39 NxRP! when 39 . . . B–N5?? will not do because of 40 QxBch winning at once.

38   . . .   B–R5!

Position after 38 Q–B3!
Black is in trouble

Diagram 13

BLACK

WHITE

Now White dare not play 39 NxRP?? because of 39 . . . B–N5 and Black wins.

39 B–N6   . . .

Threatening mate and seemingly forcing the win of the Rook Pawn.

39 . . .   BxNch

Black sees that after 40 KxB he will soon be out of his troubles: 40 . . . B–B4!; 41 BxRP (if 41 BxN, KxB; 42 B–R6 threatening to regain the Pawn, Black replies 42 . . . Q–KR1!; 43 BxN, QxBch; 44 K–R4, Q–N5ch with an easily won end-game for Black), P–K5; 42 Q–K2, NxB; 43 QxN, K–N2; 44 B–B4, B–N3; 45 Q–K2, Q–B4 and Black has a winning game.

40 PxB   B–B4!

Best. Again White can regain his Pawn but the results would not be appetizing.

Black does not fear 41 BxRP with the sequel 42 . . . NxB;

Position after 40 . . . B–B4
Black manages to hold the extra Pawn

Diagram 14

BLACK

WHITE

43 QxN, B–N5; 44 Q–R7, Q–B4 and the ending is lost for White because his Queen Pawn will become untenable.

41	BxN	KxB
42	N–K4	Q–Q2
43	B–R6	. . .

Threat: 44 NxQPch, QxN; 45 BxN, KxB; 46 QxB etc.

43	. . .	K–N3!
44	BxN	KxB

Now it will not do for White to play 45 NxQP? for then 45 . . . B–N5 wins a piece for Black.

45	P–QN4	. . .

This leads to the loss of White's Queen Pawn, but the alternative method of supporting the Queen Pawn with P–N3 and P–B4 is also not good enough to save the game: 45 P–N3, K–N3; 46 N–B2, Q–K2; 47 P–B4, P–N5; 48 K–N2, P–K5 followed by . . . Q–K4 and the steady infiltration of Black's Queen and King must decide in his favor.

45	. . .	P–B5
46	N–Q2	Q–KB2
47	Q–K3	. . .

Feeling that he must lose his artificially isolated Queen Pawn sooner or later, White heads for a series of checks that promise to be very troublesome.

Position after 47 Q–K3
White voluntarily surrenders his Queen Pawn

Diagram 15

BLACK

WHITE

47	. . .	QxP
48	Q–N5ch	B–N3
49	Q–K7ch	K–N1
50	Q–Q8ch	K–N2
51	Q–Q7ch	K–B3
52	Q–Q8ch	K–B4
53	Q–Q7ch	K–B3
54	Q–Q8ch	K–N2
55	Q–K7ch	Q–B2!

Black has had time to convince himself that the only way to win is to give up his Queen Pawn.

56   QxQP   Q–B7ch
57   K–R3   K–R3
58   N–N1   . . .

This blunder costs a piece, but he was helpless against the coming . . . P–K5. A pretty possibility: 58 Q–Q5, P–K5!; 59 NxKP, Q–KB4ch; 60 QxQ, BxQch and Black still wins a piece.

58   . . .   Q–KB4ch

Relying on the fact that the Bishop is pinned, White had overlooked this drastic check.

59   K–N2   QxN

White still has a few checks left.

60   Q–B8ch   K–N4
61   Q–Q8ch   K–N5
62   Q–Q7ch   Q–B4
63   Q–Q1ch   K–N4
         Resigns

This hard-fought game is an instructive example of this difficult variation.

GAME 2

(gives us an excellent idea of the PxP variation)

U. S. Championship Tournament, 1939

WHITE	BLACK
S. Reshevsky	W. Adams
1 P–K4	P–K4
2 N–KB3	N–QB3
3 B–N5	P–QR3
4 B–R4	N–B3
5 Castles	B–K2

6	R–K1	P–QN4
7	B–N3	P–Q3
8	P–B3	Castles
9	P–KR3	N–QR4
10	B–B2	P–B4
11	P–Q4	Q–B2
12	QN–Q2	N–B3

See Diagram 7. So far the play has been identical with that of the previous game. But now White branches off by capturing in the center.

13	PxBP!	PxP
14	N–B1	. . .

White's aim, as we know, is to play N–K3–Q5.

14	. . .	R–Q1
15	Q–K2	B–K3

Note how with his last two moves Black has played to block White's control of the coveted square. Black does not fear 16 N–N5, which he can answer effectively with 16 . . . B–B5.

16	N–K3	. . .

Preventing . . . B–B5 and therefore threatening N–N5.

(See Diagram 17)

Now that White has prevented . . . B–B5, Black ought to take the simple precaution of ruling out N–N5 by playing . . . P–R3.

An interesting alternative was 16 . . . P–B5 and if 17 N–N5, N–Q5!; 18 PxN, PxP; 19 NxB, PxN and Black recovers the piece advantageously, as he has . . . P–Q6 in reserve if need be.

16	. . .	P–N5?

This is about the worst move on the board. Black creates a fatal weakness in his Pawn position by allowing White to monopolize a vital diagonal.

17	N–N5	. . .

Black is in trouble. After 17 . . . B–Q2; 18 B–N3, B–K1

Position after 16 N–K3
Black does not measure up to the needs of the position

Diagram 16

BLACK

WHITE

(thanks to his inferior 16th move, Black cannot play 18 . . .
P–B5); 19 N–Q5 (the key move) White has a tremendous
initiative.

　　17 . . .　　　　P–QR4
　　18 NxB　　　　PxN

These doubled Pawns make an ugly impression. Perhaps
Black is comforted by the fact that his Pawn on King 3 keeps
White's pieces out of the valuable Queen 5 square.

　　19 B–N3　　　. . .

White immediately fastens on the weak spot.

　　19 . . .　　　　Q–B1
　　20 Q–B4　　　. . .

Another strong move made possible by Black's feeble 16th
move.

　　20 . . .　　　　K–B2
　　21 P–QR4!　　. . .

By ruling out . . . P–R5, White keeps his King Bishop on the vital diagonal.

21   . . .   P–N3
22   N–N4   . . .

White threatens to win a Pawn by 23 QxKPch!, QxQ; 24 N–R6ch etc.

22   . . .   NxN
23   PxN   N–N1

Position after 23 . . . N–N1
How does White step up the attack?

Diagram 17

BLACK

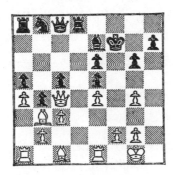

WHITE

24   P–B4!   . . .

White opens the King Bishop file for a decisive onslaught on the Black King.

24   . . .   KPxP
25   BxP   Q–R3

On other moves White's attack crashes through rapidly, for example 25 . . . N–R3; 26 R–KB1, K–N2; 27 B–K5ch, K–R3; 28 Q–K2 and White has a mating attack.

            26   R–KB1   QxQ
Black vainly pins his hopes to the exchange of Queens.
            27   BxQ   K–N2
            28   B–K5ch   K–R3
            29   R–B7   . . .
This leaves Black without a good move, 29 . . . R–K1 being
refuted by 30 B–N5—or even 30 K–B2 threatening the deadly
R–R1ch.

On 29 . . . B–B1 White wins with 30 B–B6, R–K1; 31
P–N5ch, K–R4; 32 B–K2ch, K–R5; 33 K–B2 etc.

One of the most interesting possibilities is 29 . . . N–B3; 30
P–N5ch!, BxP; 31 B–N7ch, K–R4; 32 B–K2ch, K–R5; 33 K–R2,
B–K2; 34 RxB, NxR; 35 B–B6ch, P–N4; 36 P–N3 mate.
            29   . . .   B–Q3
            30   B–N7ch   Resigns
Black cannot face 30 . . . K–N4; 31 B–B6ch winning a Rook.
A good example of the way in which the PxP variation can
bowl over an unsuspecting opponent.

Some useful pointers

For White:

1. Attempt to "encircle" the enemy.
2. Utilize superior mobility in various ways.
3. Build up a King-side attack.
4. Make use of the open Queen Rook file.
5. Exploit Black's Queen-side weaknesses.
6. Set up an ideal Pawn center (Pawns at King 4 and Queen
4).
7. Refute premature counterattacks.

For Black:

1. Rely on a solid position for pure defensive play.
2. Seek counterattack in the P–Q5 variation with . . . P–KB4.

3. Look for counterattack on the Queen Rook file (as in Game 1).

4. Take advantage of any inaccuracies in White's building up of the attack.

Conclusions

Undoubtedly Black gets an even game from these variations. Yet he cannot rely on this theoretical verdict. For White has a choice of several procedures, so that Black must be patient, vigilant, and foresighted. We therefore conclude that Black may be better off with the Sicilian Defense or French Defense or even the Caro-Kann Defense or Alekhine's Defense. These lines of play will form the subject matter of the following lessons.

Lesson 2

SICILIAN DEFENSE

(Scheveningen Variation)

WHITE	BLACK
1 P–K4	P–QB4

This is Black's most aggressive reply. It leads to a rich full game with chances for both sides.

Characteristic situation of the Sicilian Defense

Diagram 1

BLACK

WHITE

The normal course of the variation

This variation is made up of the following moves:

WHITE	BLACK
1 P–K4	P–QB4
2 N–KB3	. . .

The most popular move for White. Another system of development goes like this: 2 N–QB3, N–QB3; 3 P–KN3, P–KN3; 4 B–N2, B–N2; 5 P–Q3, P–Q3. This system leads to a close game—in which there is a great deal of jockeying and maneuvering before the opposing forces come into contact with each other.

The variation we are about to study is quite different. The position opens up more rapidly and the contact between the forces is much sharper and more critical.

2 . . .	P–Q3
3 P–Q4	. . .

An important move for White. It opens up the game for his pieces and gives him ample scope for development.

3 . . .	PxP

There is little choice here for Black, as he does not want White's Pawn center to become too powerful.

4 NxP	N–KB3
5 N–QB3	N–B3

Even at this early stage we can forecast some of the strategical possibilities for both sides.

Before studying this variation in detail, we can forecast that the half-open Queen file will be an important base of operations for White, and that the Queen 4 square will serve as a valuable central post for White's minor pieces, particularly a Knight.

Black, on the other hand, will concentrate on the half-open Queen Bishop file for his Queen and Rooks. Here the outpost square will be Black's Queen Bishop 5, and Black will try to establish a Knight on this square by . . . N–QR4–QB5 or . . . N–K4–QB5.

Position after 5 . . . N–B3
What are some of the strategical objectives?

Diagram 2

BLACK

WHITE

6 B–K2   P–K3

This is really the basic move of the variation, as far as Black is concerned. It looks strange because it blocks the natural diagonal of Black's Queen Bishop. But later discussion will expound the reasons for this move.

7 Castles   P–QR3

Another move of basic significance. Black wants to play . . . Q–B2 (in line with his policy of pressure on the Queen Bishop file). So he first rules out the possibility of his Queen's being harried by a White Knight going to Queen Knight 5.

8 B–K3   Q–B2
9 P–B4   . . .

An important move for White. It prepares for future aggressive action by way of P–K5 or P–B5 (at the proper time) and also holds out the promise of a Pawn-storming attack in conjunction with P–KN4.

9 . . .   B–K2

Black continues his development. We have now gone far enough to be able to examine the basic ideas underlying Black's somewhat strange-looking development.

Position after 9 . . . B–K2
Characteristic position in the variation

Diagram 3

BLACK

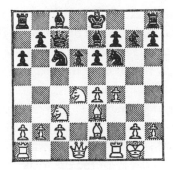

WHITE

A preliminary study of the position gives us the feeling that Black's position is very cramped. Why then does he choose it?

Philosophic basis of the defense

In most games beginning with 1 P–K4, the reply is 1 . . . P–K4. This *may* be the very best reply, from a coldly objective standpoint. But there are psychological aspects to be considered as well.

Suppose Black chooses a different first move. Then he is bucking White's desire to bring about a certain position; Black is bringing on a clash of opposed wills.

To repeat: 1 . . . P–K4 is an almost automatic response. It may be due to habit or to ignorance of a feasible alternative. But in that case White can carry out his preconceived ideas. He may obtain a violent attack by playing a gambit; or he may obtain positional pressure with an opening on the order of the Ruy Lopez; or he may pursue a dull draw with the Four Knights' Game or the Giuoco Pianissimo.

Actually it does not much matter just what particular opening White plays. It is enough for us to know that he is playing what he likes, whereas Black may not like it at all.

Any of the so-called "irregular" replies, on the other hand, lead to a totally different kind of play. White can no longer proceed according to his own intentions. This time it is Black who dictates the character of the play. The curious thing is that although Black remains a move behind he may be said to have the initiative!

The Scheveningen Variation of the Sicilian Defense is one such "irregular" reply. It leads to a rich game full of complications and chances for both sides. To play it with understanding, however, you must be familiar with the theory of the center on which it is predicated.

The two theories of Pawn control of the center

According to the classical theory, the center should be controlled by direct occupation. Thus, after 1 P–K4, P–K4 we have an example of occupational control by both King Pawns. White tries by an immediate of subsequent P–KB4 or P–Q4 to remove the Black King Pawn. If Black exchanges Pawns (. . . KPxP) he is said "to give up the center." The upshot is supposed to be greater mobility for White. On the other hand, if Black refuses to capture and supports his King Pawn with another Pawn, he is said "to hold the center." This generally gives him a somewhat cramped but solid game.

The hypermodern theory, contrariwise, is based on the idea of remote control of the center. The claim here is that instead of occupying the center directly the players should aim to control it by applying pressure from the wings. (This is dealt with in more detail in Lesson 8.) That is why such moves as . . . P–QB4 and . . . P–KB4 are so popular in modern master play.

The Sicilian Defense falls into the hypermodern realm. By answering 1 P–K4 with 1 . . . P–QB4 Black tries to control the center from the wing. At the same time he reaps the additional psychological advantage of confronting White with unusual and possibly distasteful tasks.

Normal Pawn Skeleton

Diagram 4

BLACK

WHITE

White's Normal Formation

White's King Rook Pawn remains at its original square, except in the case of Pawn-storming attacks on the King-side. Once the King Bishop Pawn and the King Knight Pawn have advanced, the King Rook Pawn may join them by advancing P–KR4.

White's *King Knight Pawn* may often follow up the advance of his King Bishop Pawn by P–KN4 and P–KN5. The object is to drive off Black's best defensive piece (his King Knight) and also to cramp Black's game generally.

However, this advance is not to be undertaken lightly. If it fails—as it does in the first Illustrative Game—it is likely to leave White with a compromised Pawn position full of weaknesses.

White's *King Bishop Pawn* plays to King Bishop 4 early in the game. This serves a variety of purposes. It gives White control of the important central square King 5. It therefore prevents the Black pieces from using that square; for example, . . . N–K4 is ruled out.

Another purpose of P–KB4 is to prepare an aggressive advance—P–K5 or P–KB5. It is in the nature of these advances that they can be very effective when well prepared, or may recoil on White if ill prepared. In addition, as we have seen, P–KB4 may be the prelude to a Pawn-storming attack. Finally, P–KB4 serves the general purpose of giving White's King-side pieces more maneuvering room.

White's *King Pawn* plays to King 4 on the first move. This Pawn is always on the alert to advance to King 5, driving away Black's King Knight. This latter objective almost always relates to a projected King-side attack.

Another point to P–K5 is that it opens up the diagonal of White's Bishop at King Bishop 3. With the Bishop trained on Black's Queen-side, P–K5 implies Queen-side action on White's part.

White's *Queen Pawn* advances to Queen 4 and is exchanged for Black's Queen Bishop Pawn. As already explained, this opens up White's Queen 4 square as a base of operations.

White's *Queen Bishop Pawn* remains at Queen Bishop 2. White must keep in mind at all times that this Pawn is the indirect target of Black's pressure along the half-open Queen Bishop file.

White's *Queen Knight Pawn* remains on Queen Knight 2 to protect the White Knight at Queen Bishop 3. Remember that this Knight is the direct target of Black's pressure along the half-open Queen Bishop file. Sometimes it is very tempting for White to play P–QN3 to eject an annoying Black Knight which is occupying the outpost square Queen Bishop 5. But this temptation should be resisted, because it renders White highly vulnerable on the Queen Bishop file.

White's *Queen Rook Pawn* generally plays to Queen Rook 4 at a fairly early stage. One of the objectives of . . . P–QR3 is to continue . . . P–QN4—when feasible—in order to fianchetto the Black Queen Bishop. (. . . P–QN4 has other purposes as well, as you will see under the discussion of Black's Queen Knight 4).

Once White has advanced P–QR4, he threatens to play P–R5, creating a serious "hole" on Black's Queen Knight 3 square, which has been weakened by . . . P–QR3. This is illustrated in Diagram 5.

Black's Queen Knight 3 square is a "hole"

Diagram 5

BLACK

WHITE

In such a situation as the one shown in Diagram 5, White oftens obtains a decisive positional advantage by observing or even occupying Black's weakened Queen Knight 3 square with one of his Knights or his Queen Bishop.

As for White's pieces:

White's *King Knight* plays to King Bishop 3 in the opening and then reaches Queen 4 as a result of the early exchange of Pawns. Later on this Knight often goes to Queen Knight 3, partly to avoid a simplifying exchange, partly to maintain a grip on the Queen Rook 5 square.

White's *Queen Knight* plays to Queen Bishop 3, where its chief function is to stop Black from playing . . . P–Q4 advantageously. Where a successful King-side attack is indicated, White may be able to continue N–K4 after P–K5. This leads to a highly effective concentration of White's forces on the King-side.

White's *King Bishop* can play to Queen 3 or even Queen Bishop 4, but the best move of all is B–K2. Later on, after P–KB4, the Bishop will go to King Bishop 3, where it exerts strong pressure along the diagonal, particularly by way of restraining Black from freeing himself with . . . P–Q4.

An alternative method of deploying the Bishop is to play B–Q3 (after N–N3) with a view to P–K5, when the presence of the Bishop on the mighty attacking diagonal should give White a powerful King-side attack.

White's *Queen Bishop* plays to King 3, where it supports White's Knight at Queen 4 and is well placed for action on either wing.

White's *King Rook* is effectively posted at King Bishop 1 after castling. Here it supports the advance of White's King Bishop Pawn—in some cases to King Bishop 6. In some cases—particularly in the event of a Pawn-storming attack characterized by P–KN4–5, this Rook may be usefully employed at King Knight 1.

White's *Queen Rook* goes to Queen 1 after the White Queen's removal from that square. The Rook is well posted on this half-open file.

White's *Queen* should go to the "pivot square" King 1. Then if Queen-side action is intended, White can follow up with Q–KB2. On the other hand, if White contemplates action on the King-side, Q–KN3 is indicated. The participation of White's Queen in the attack is particularly menacing because Black's Queen is not directly involved in the defense. Another virtue of Q–KN3 is that it threatens P–K5, appreciably strengthening the force of White's attack.

White's *King* goes to King Rook 1 as a rule. This avoids potentially dangerous pins along the diagonal King Knight 1–Queen Rook 7. It also serves as a useful preparation for the Pawn-storming advance P–KN4–5.

Black's Normal Formation

Black's *King Rook Pawn, King Knight Pawn* and *King Bishop Pawn* should all remain unmoved. In any event, Black should avoid moving any of these Pawns unless he is absolutely forced to do so. Any advance of these Pawns will merely create a target for White's Pawn-storming attack and make it that more effective.

Black's *King Pawn* plays to King 3, where it supports a later . . . P–Q4. Sometimes the King Pawn advances to King 4 in the middle game, but only if a direct advantage is involved, as . . . P–K4 creates a "hole" at Black's Queen 4 square.

Black's *Queen Pawn* goes to Queen 3 in the opening. Thus his King Pawn and Queen Pawn take up a strong defensive position in the center. Later on Black may succeed in playing . . . P–Q4, opening up his position for stronger placement of his forces. Diagrams 6a and 6b illustrate the consequences of advancing the King Pawn or the Queen Pawn.

Characteristic position after . . . P–K4

Diagram 6a

BLACK

WHITE

Characteristic position after . . . P–Q4

Diagram 6b

BLACK

WHITE

Examining Diagram 6a, you can see that Black has created a hole at his Q4 square. White's strategy will be to reply PxP or

P–B5 followed by B–N5. The idea is to eliminate Black's King Knight (which bears on the critical Queen 4 square). Once this is done, White can concentrate on the vital square. He may occupy it with a Knight, and he may also double Rooks on the Queen file to menace Black's backward Queen Pawn.

After a well prepared . . . P–Q4 Black's pieces suddenly spring to life as his King Knight, Queen Bishop and a Rook on the Queen file all cooperate for more intensified pressure on the center. The course of the game will take a radically different course depending on whether White replies PxP or P–K5. If White replies PxP, he greatly increases the mobility of Black's pieces without obtaining any compensating advantage. If on the other hand White plays P–K5, Black replies . . . N–K5. In that case a sharp struggle results: Black has gained ground in the center, White has prospects of King-side attack.

Black's *Queen Bishop Pawn* plays to Queen Bishop 4 on the first move and soon thereafter captures White's Queen Pawn. This gives Black a half-open Queen Bishop file for his Queen and Rooks; and here we have the basis for most of Black's strategy.

Black's *Queen Knight Pawn* should if at all possible advance to Queen Knight 4. (At this point you might review what was written about White's Queen Rook Pawn.) To recapitulate, this advance of the Queen Knight makes room for the fianchetto of Black's Queen Bishop at Queen Knight 2; it intensifies Black's hold on the invasion square Queen Bishop 5; it threatens . . . P–N5 (driving off White's Queen Knight) in some instances and thus adds to the effectiveness of Black's operations on the half-open Queen Bishop file.

As we have seen, White sometimes prevents . . . P–QN4 by anticipating it with P–QR4. What then? Well, Black has a choice of two procedures: one is to play . . . P–QN3 (*before* White's P–QR5). This avoids a hole at Black's Queen Knight 3 square and also prepares the development of Black's Queen Bishop at Queen Knight 2. On the other hand, Black has a somewhat burdensome task protecting his Pawn on Queen Knight 3 if White attacks it with his Queen Bishop (on King 3) and his Queen (on King Bishop 2).

The other way for Black to develop his Queen Bishop is to play . . . B–Q2, leaving his Queen Knight Pawn unmoved. This second method leaves Black with a somewhat crowded but solid position full of resources, as we shall see in the first Illustrative Game.

Black's *Queen Rook Pawn*, as we know, goes to Queen Rook 3 to protect Black's Queen (at Queen Bishop 2) from attacks via N–QN5. Another reason for . . . P–QR3 is that it prepares for . . . P–QN4.

As for Black's pieces:

Black's *King Knight* always goes to King Bishop 3. Here it serves as the best bulwark Black has against a possible King-side attack by White. In addition the Knight plays an important role in the struggle for center control (see the discussion of Diagram 6b).

Black's *Queen Knight* plays to Queen Bishop 3 and its most important assignment is to establish itself as an outpost at Queen Bishop 5 on the half-open Queen Bishop file. Diagram 8 shows a typical position:

The Black Knight at the advanced outpost is a thorn in White's side. At Queen Bishop 5 the Knight is sometimes in a position to continue . . . NxB when White's Queen Bishop is at King 3. Such a capture would give Black the advantage of two active Bishops against Bishop and Knight. (Even so, Black may decide that holding on to his outpost is still more advantageous.)

Even more irritating for White is Black's threat against the White Queen Knight Pawn after . . . N–QB5. To guard a mere Pawn with a Rook is not inviting. To capture the invading

Characteristic position with Black outpost established on
Queen Bishop 5

Diagram 7

BLACK

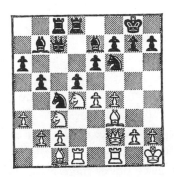

WHITE

Knight is hardly a solution, as Black simply recaptures . . . QxB and the pressure on the Queen Bishop file continues undiminished. It will therefore be seen that Black's establishment of the outpost on Queen Bishop 5 is a great strategical trump.

Black's *King Bishop* plays to King 2 in the opening. This piece has little scope for a long time to come, as it is blocked by the Black Pawn on Queen 3. But this stodgy appearance is deceptive, because the Bishop provides valuable defensive resources. In addition, the successful execution of . . . P–Q4 will suddenly bring this Bishop to life.

An additional point about . . . P–K4 (already discussed under Black's King Pawn): this advance will reduce the mobility of the King Bishop, and reduce it to the humdrum task of defending Black's backward Queen Pawn.

In cases of particularly sharp attack by White, Black may usefully retreat his King Bishop to King Bishop 1. This protects his King Knight 2 square and also aids in opening up the second rank for protection of the King-side by Black's Queen at Queen Bishop 2.

Black's *Queen Bishop* is fianchettoed at Queen Knight 2, from where it strikes along the long diagonal and prepares for an eventual . . . P–Q4. As we have seen, it is not always possible or desirable to play . . . B–QN2. In such cases, Black must content himself with . . . B–Q2. Here the Bishop (like his colleague at King 2) contributes usefully to the general solidity of Black's position. Later on in the game the Bishop may get to Queen Bishop 3 or Queen Knight 4 (aggressive) or King 1 (defensive). This rearrangement has the virtue of allowing a Black Rook at Queen 1 to support the thrust . . . P–Q4.

Black's *King Rook* often goes to Queen 1 to defend the Queen Pawn or prepare for . . . P–Q4. The Rook move also has the virtue of leaving Black's pieces more maneuvering space on the King-side for defensive purposes.

Black's *Queen Rook* goes almost invariably to Queen Bishop 1 to contribute to Black's pressure on the half-open Queen Bishop file, with White's Queen Bishop Pawn as the potential target. The psychological value of this pressure on the Queen Bishop file is that it makes it impossible for White to mark time. Sooner or later he is goaded into action which may often be ill advised. In such cases Black can often react with decisive counterplay.

Black's *Queen* goes to the ideal square Queen Bishop 2, beginning the pressure on the half-open Queen Bishop file. But this is not all: at Queen Bishop 2 Black's Queen helps to restrain White's P–K5; the Queen also guards vital squares (particularly Black's Queen Knight 3), and sometimes undertakes aggressive action on the Queen-side with . . . Q–QB5.

Black's *King* goes to King Knight 1 as part of King-side castling. Sometimes, in the case of a particularly heavy attack, the King may play to King Rook 1 to make room for the retreat . . . N–KN1. But this is a measure that should be undertaken only in extreme situations.

ILLUSTRATIVE GAMES

GAME 1

(in which Black thrusts back a formidable-looking attack)

New York, 1928

WHITE	BLACK
C. Jaffe	F. Reinfeld
1 P–K4	P–QB4
2 N–KB3	N–QB3
3 P–Q4	PxP
4 NxP	N–B3
5 N–QB3	P–Q3
6 B–K2	P–K3
7 B–K3	B–K2
8 Q–Q2	. . .

Position after 8 Q–Q2
White's play lacks precision

Diagram 8

BLACK

WHITE

With his last move White has deviated from the approved sequence. After the Queen move White will still be able to play Q–KB2 later on. But if he had castled first and then played P–B4, he could continue with Q–K1–N3—the strongest development available to the White Queen.

Of course this is only an inexactitude—not a blunder. It is by no means fatal. But a succession of such seemingly trifling mistakes often leads to disaster.

$$8 \ldots \quad \text{P–QR3}$$
$$9 \ \text{P–B4} \quad \ldots$$

The postponement of castling is another curious point. We get the impression that White knows the moves but doesn't much care which order he plays them in.

$$9 \ldots \quad \text{B–Q2}$$

Black too does not find the most accurate order—9 . . . Q–B2 in the hope of being able to fianchetto his Queen Bishop.

$$10 \ \text{R–Q1} \quad \ldots$$

Again the order is clumsy. Somewhere hereabouts White should be thinking of P–QR4, restraining Black from advancing . . . P–QN4.

$$10 \ldots \quad \text{Q–B2}$$
$$11 \ \text{Castles} \quad \text{R–QB1}$$
$$12 \ \text{N–N3} \quad \text{P–QN4}$$

An important thematic move, as we know. And in addition the threat of . . . P–N5 (winning White's King Pawn) is unpleasant.

(See Diagram 9)

The simplest way for White to give additional protection to his King Pawn is 13 B–B3.

$$13 \ \text{P–QR3?} \quad \ldots$$

This perfectly plausible move prevents . . . P–N5 and therefore seems excellent. The trouble is that the move creates a target for Black's later Pawn-storming advance along the Queen Knight

Position after 12 . . . P–QN4
How should White guard his King Pawn?

Diagram 9

BLACK

WHITE

file. The consequences of White's mistake will be most instructive.

| 13 | . . . | Castles |
| 14 | B–B3 | KR–Q1 |

To an inexperienced player Black's position looks cramped, and so it is. The important point is that Black's position has a great deal of staying power and latent counterattacking possibilities.

| 15 | Q–B2 | . . . |

Threatening to win the exchange with B–N6, but Black has a good reply which is quite obvious.

| 15 | . . . | R–N1 |

This parries the threat, at the cost of renouncing the thematic procedure of exploiting the Queen Bishop file. But there are times—and this is one of them—when a player has to depart from hidebound rules. As it happens, Black has ample compensation: he plans . . . P–QR4 followed by . . . P–N5, with a strong Queen-side initiative.

16   P–N4   . . .

Naturally White is not content to remain passive. He embarks
on a King-side demonstration which is less menacing than it
looks.

Position after 16 P–N4
How does Black combine attack and defense?

Diagram 10

BLACK

WHITE

16 . . .   B–K1!

This retreat strengthens the defense of Black's King-side and
at the same time makes room for the retreat of Black's King
Knight to Queen 2. One would think that Black is on the run,
but once his King Knight gets to Queen 2 he will be on the point
of playing . . . N–N3–B5. If this maneuver succeeds, Black will
have carried out his prime strategical objective.

17   P–N5   N–Q2
18   P–KR4   N–N3!

This really "puts the question" to White. After 19 K–N2,
N–B5; 20 B–B1 he has avoided the exchange of Queens—only

to find that 20 . . . P–QR4! gives Black a marked initiative because of the threat of . . . P–N5.

White therefore decides to remove the troublesome Knight at
once—at the cost, however, of ceding Black the powerful Bishop-
pair. And Black has other assets too: his coming Queen-side initiative with . . . P–QR4 and his pressure on White's Pawns.

    19 BxN   QxB

Now White's "attack"—such as it was—is over, and the initiative remains in Black's hands.

    20 QxQ   RxQ
    21 N–K2   R–B1!

The old theme of pressure on the half-open file.

    22 P–B3   . . .

White suffers from the dilemma of making perfectly reasonable moves which nevertheless add up to serious trouble. What
this indicates, of course, is that his position is basically inferior.

    22 . . .   P–QR4!

Position after 22 . . . P–QR4!
Black plans a break-through

Diagram 11

BLACK

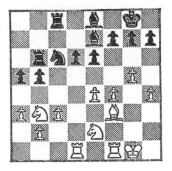

WHITE

Black cannot be prevented from opening at least one file with . . . P–N5 and thus enabling his Rooks to come to grips with the weakened White Pawns.

         23   N/K2–Q4 NxN
         24   RxN   . . .

The alternative 24 PxN, P–N5!; 25 N–R1, PxP; 26 PxP, R–N7; 27 R–B2, R/B1–N1 is anything but inviting for White.

         24 . . .   P–N5!

At last the long awaited advance is in order. White cannot very well answer 25 NxP because of 25 . . . PxRP; 26 PxP, R–N4; 27 N–B4, . . . P–K4! and Black wins a piece. Or 26 P–N4, RxBP with the winning threat of . . . P–Q4.

         25   BPxP   PxP
         26   PxP   . . .

Here 26 RxNP, RxR; 27 PxR, R–N1 amounts to the same thing.

         26 . . .   R/B1–N1
         27   N–Q2   RxP
         28   RxR   RxR
         29   P–N3   . . .

         (See Diagram 12)

         29 . . .   R–Q5!

A very important move. Now that Black has succeeded in getting his Rook to the fifth rank, he gains time by attacking the Knight to enforce . . . P–Q4. In due course this will lead to the massacre of White's King-side Pawns.

         30   R–Q1   P–Q4!

This leaves White helpless, as Black threatens . . . B–N5; and 31 PxP is answered by 31 . . . RxBP.

         31   N–B1   . . .

White gives up a Pawn—not that he can help himself—in the hope of regaining it later on.

Position after 29 P–N3
Black prepares for . . . P Q4!

Diagram 12

BLACK

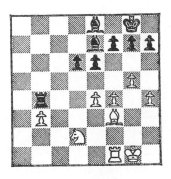

WHITE

31	. . .	RxR
32	BxR	PxP
33	N–N3	B–B4ch

Now the Bishops come into play very strongly.

34	K–B1	B–N4ch
35	B–K2	B–B3
36	B–B4	B–Q3!

This soon seals the fate of White's Bishop Pawn.

37	N–K2	P–K6

In order to make room for his Queen Bishop.

38	N–Q4	B–K5
39	N–K2	B–B6
40	K–N1	. . .

Or 40 N–Q4, B–KN5 and the Bishop Pawn bites the dust.

40	. . .	BxN
41	BxB	BxP

Mission accomplished. White still hopes to draw with the

Bishops on opposite colors, but the two extra Pawns are too much for him to contend against.

42	K–N2	B–B2
43	K–B3	B–N3
44	P–N4	P–R3
45	K–K4	K–B1
46	K–B4	K–K2
47	K–K5	PxP
48	PxP	P–B3ch
49	PxPch	PxPch

Black has liquidated the White Pawns, leaving a cluster of irresistible Black Pawns.

50	K–B4	K–Q3

Position after 50 . . . K–Q3
White is helpless

Diagram 13

BLACK

WHITE

White resigns, and quite rightly so. A plausible continuation would be 51 B–B4, P–B4; 52 P–N5 (if 52 K–B3, P–K4 and

Black is bound to penetrate), K–B4!; 53 B–K2 (if 53 BxP??, P–K7 and the Pawn queens), K–Q5, 54 B–B1, B–B2ch, 55 K–B3, P–K4 winning easily. For example, 56 B–K2, P–K5ch; 57 K–N2, P–B5, etc.

This game is a good example of the resources available to Black in this complex variation.

GAME 2

(shows how White can make the best of his theoretical chances)

Tiflis, 1937

WHITE	BLACK
G. *Levenfish*	V. *Makogonov*
1 P–K4	P–QB4
2 N–KB3	P–K3
3 P–Q4	PxP
4 NxP	N–KB3
5 N–QB3	P–Q3
6 B–K2	P–QR3
7 Castles	Q–B2
8 P–QR4	. . .

This is more alert than White's play in the previous game.

(See Diagram 14)

8	. . .	N–B3
9	B–K3	B–K2
10	P–B4	Castles
11	N–N3	. . .

White threatens 12 P–R5, establishing Black's Queen Knight 3 square as an irreparable hole.

Position after 8 P–QR4
White has prevented . . . P–QN4

Diagram 14

BLACK

WHITE

| 11 | . . . | P–QN3 |

Black forestalls P–R5 and also prepares to develop his Queen
Bishop at Queen Knight 2.

| 12 | B–B3 | B–N2 |
| 13 | Q–K1 | . . . |

Again in contrast to the previous game, White brings his
Queen to the most effective square.

| 13 | . . . | KR–K1 |

This is not much of a contribution. Perhaps 13 . . . N–QN5;
14 R–B1, P–Q4 was more to the point.

14	R–Q1	N–Q2
15	Q–N3	B–KB1
16	R–B2!	. . .

Very well played. White is now ready to double his Rooks on
the King Bishop file or Queen file as circumstances may dictate.

| 16 | . . . | N–B4 |

In contrast to White's purposeful building up of his position, Black merely drifts.

17   P–B5!   . . .

The attack begins. White's immediate threat is 18 NxN, NPxN; 19 BxP winning a Pawn because the Queen Pawn is pinned. Another threat is 18 P–B6, P–N3; 19 Q–R4 followed by B–R6 and White has a mating attack on King Knight 7 in mind.

17 . . .   N–K4

In a cramped position the defender should seek simplifying exchanges, hence 17 . . . NxN is in order.

On the other hand, 17 . . . PxP is unsatisfactory because of 18 BxN, NPxB; 19 NxP, which leaves White with a very strong game.

Position after 17 . . . N–K4
White builds up the attack

Diagram 15

BLACK

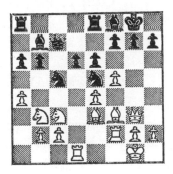

WHITE

18   N–Q4!   . . .

White prevents the exchange which would have eased Black's game somewhat.

Meanwhile the menace of P–B6 has become more acute. White has in mind the possibility of 19 P–B6, P–N3; 20 Q–R4 and again White threatens a mating attack beginning with B–R6.

18 . . .   K–R1

Black takes steps against P–B6.

19 B–N5   . . .

White renews the nasty threat of P–B6.

19 . . .   B–K2

Black parries the threat of P–B6 once more.

20 B–R5!   . . .

This very fine move, intended to provoke a new weakness in the form of . . . P–N3, threatens to win a Pawn with 21 PxP.

Nor is White concerned about 20 . . . NxKP; 21 NxN, BxN; 22 PxP and White still wins a Pawn.

20 . . .   Q–Q1
21 BxB   . . .

A very important exchange for White, as Black's weak Queen Pawn is now stripped of its most useful protection. This appears in the variation 21 . . . QxB; 22 PxP, NxP/K3; 23 N–B5 winning the Queen Pawn.

21 . . .   RxB
22 PxP   PxP

(See Diagram 16)

23 N–B3!   . . .

Simple, obvious, and very strong. The point is that Black's Knight at King 4, the key to his position, must now disappear.

23 . . .   NxNch

Or 23 . . . Q–B2; 24 NxN, PxN; 25 R/Q1–KB1, Q–N1; 26 QxKP! and White wins without much trouble.

24 BxN   P–K4
25 R/B2–Q2 . . .

Position after 22 . . . PxP
White finds the positionally decisive move

Diagram 16

BLACK

WHITE

An impossible move to meet satisfactorily, for if 25 . . . R–Q2; 26 B–N4 and Black's Rook is driven off from the defense.

  25 . . .   R–K3
  26 P–N4! . . .

Forcing a clumsy retreat of the Black Knight which blocks the protection of the weak Queen Pawn.

  26 . . .   N–Q2
  27 B–N4! R–B3
  28 RxP   Resigns

The pin on the Queen file leaves Black helpless. A beautifully played game by White.

Some useful pointers

For White:

 1. Play P–QR4 to prevent . . . P–QN4.

 2. Prevent an eventual . . . P–Q4 by concentrating enough pieces to make the advance impossible or disadvantageous.

3. Make up your mind fairly early whether you want to play Q–K1–N3 or advance the three King-side wing Pawns for a Pawn-storming attack.

4. Try to create a hole at Black's Queen Knight 3 square.

For Black:

1. Above all, try to establish a Knight at your Queen Bishop 5 square.

2. Strive for . . . P–Q4 in order to get a firmer foothold in the center and open up the game for your pieces.

3. Be careful to avoid a hole at your Queen Knight 3 square.

4. Don't allow yourself to be boxed into a purely defensive position.

Conclusions

This is a defense that calls for patience, unruffled calm, alertness, and good position judgment. These are hardly qualities that one can expect from the inexperienced player. Yet he can reasonably hope to develop them by specializing in this defense, which calls for maneuvering on both wings, skillful defensive play, foreseeing the character of possible endgames. This complex defense is a miniature study of chess itself in all its myriad forms.

Lesson 3

FRENCH DEFENSE

(3 P–K5 Variation)

WHITE	BLACK
1 P–K4	P–K3

Despite its conservative appearance, this hardy and resourceful defense really heralds a stern duel for control of the center.

Characteristic situation of the French Defense

Diagram 1

BLACK

WHITE

The standard continuation is:

| 2 | P–Q4 | P–Q4 |

White must advance or exchange his King Pawn or protect it. He chooses the first alternative:

3   P–K5   . . .

Position after 3 P–K5
The Basic Position

Diagram 2

BLACK

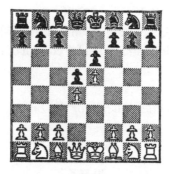

WHITE

This advance leads to two possible variations, which we shall call (a) the Pawn-Chain Variation and (b) the Centralization Variation.

Definition of terms

These terms need defining. A Pawn-Chain is a group of Pawns on adjacent squares in diagonal formation, interlocking with a similar formation of hostile Pawns. In Diagram 2, for example, White's King Pawn and Queen Pawn and Black's King Pawn and Queen Pawn make up a Pawn-Chain.

The Pawn in the rear is called a "base." In Diagram 2, White's

Queen Pawn is the base of his Pawn-Chain, while Black's King Pawn is the base of *his* Pawn-Chain.

Centralization is the situation of a piece on a central square, generally with the result that the piece gains enormously in range and mobility. The placing of a White Knight on King 5 is an example of centralization.

Why is this defense popular?

For over a century 1 . . . P–K3 has been one of the most popular replies to 1 P–K4. Many of the greatest masters have had a special fondness for it. Among the chief reasons for this favorable attitude are:

1. Black's strong, compact Pawn formation enables him to repulse premature and ill-organized attacks with ease.

2. In pursuing his aggressive intentions, White may compromise his own position. For example:

WHITE	BLACK
1 P–K4	P–K3
2 P–Q4	P–Q4
3 P–K5	. . .

With this move White announces that he intends to cramp Black's game. In particular, Black's Queen Bishop will be hard put to it to find a good square.

3 . . .	P–QB4!

A powerful reaction. Black attacks the base of White's Pawn-Chain.

4 P–QB3	. . .

White supports the base of his Pawn-Chain.

4 . . .	N–QB3

Black continues the pressure on the base of White's Pawn-Chain.

5 P–KB4?	. . .

White strives to lend added support to the foremost Pawn of his Pawn-Chain (his King Pawn); but now he overreaches himself.

Position after 5 P–KB4?
White has overextended himself

Diagram 3

BLACK

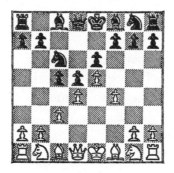

WHITE

Retribution comes quickly.

<blockquote>
5   . . .   PxP
6   PxP   Q–N3!
</blockquote>

Black renews the attack on the base of White's Pawn-Chain, which this time has no defending Pawn.

<blockquote>
7   N–KB3   N–R3!
</blockquote>

Now Black threatens 8 . . . N–B4, intensifying the attack on White's Queen Pawn. It is very doubtful whether White can avoid the loss of a Pawn. In any event Black has the initiative. This is a good example of Black's technique in beating off premature attacks.

3. It often happens that after the middle-game stage Black can look forward to having a superior endgame position.

The normal course of the variation

(a) The Pawn-Chain Variation

WHITE	BLACK
1 P–K4	P–K3
2 P–Q4	P–Q4
3 P–K5	. . .

As we know, this is a bold attempt on White's part to cramp Black's game. Black must react energetically: he must try to break up White's imposing-looking Pawn center with . . . P–QB4 and/or . . . P–KB3.

3 . . .   P–QB4!

Immediately attacking the base of White's Pawn-Chain.

4 P–QB3   . . .

White supports the base of his Pawn-Chain. We now have an inkling of the strategy for both sides: Black will try to break up the Pawn-Chain, White will give it all the protection he can.

4 . . .   N–QB3!

More pressure on the base of White's Pawn-Chain.

5 N–KB3   . . .

White protects the base of his Pawn-Chain.

5 . . .   Q–N3!

Black reinforces the pressure.

6 B–Q3?!   . . .

(See Diagram 4)

Since this Bishop really belongs at King 2, White would have been wiser to play 6 B–K2 directly.

But White has set a trap: 6 . . . PxP; 7 PxP, NxQP? (in his eagerness to confiscate the base of the Pawn-Chain, Black over-

Position after 6 B–Q3?!
White sets a feeble trap

Diagram 4

BLACK

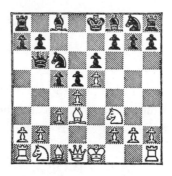

WHITE

looks a tactical finesse); 8 NxN, QxN??; 9 B–QN5ch and White
wins the Queen.

What is interesting about this trap is that it shows how inexperienced players concentrate on an idea to the exclusion of
other factors that may be of vital importance.

      6 . . .   PxP!

      7 PxP   B–Q2!

Black is on his guard. Having prevented the check by White's
Bishop, he is now ready to capture Black's King Pawn.

      8 B–K2   . . .

White's King Bishop must retreat in order to afford his Queen
Pawn adequate protection. Result: White has clearly lost a move.

      8 . . .   KN–K2!

Now you can form a judgment as to the difference between
the two Pawn-Chains. The base of Black's chain (his King
Pawn) is perfectly secure. The base of White's chain (his Queen
Pawn), on the other hand, cannot be guarded by a Pawn. Black

has the initiative. In fact, he is already threatening to win a Pawn by . . . N–B4.

Position after 8 . . . KN–K2!
White is hard put to it to protect his threatened Queen Pawn

Diagram 5

BLACK

WHITE

9	P–QN3	N–B4
10	B–N2	B–N5ch!

An excellent move. The point is that any interposition will lose the Queen Pawn for White. Consequently he must forfeit his castling privilege.

11 K–B1 . . .

And now Black has a number of good plans. See the second Illustrative Game for the likely sequel.

(b) The Centralization Variation

1	P–K4	P–K3
2	P–Q4	P–Q4
3	P–K5	P–QB4!

4 P–QB3   N–QB3!
5 N–KB3   Q–N3!

Now it would be poor policy for White to continue 6 PxP, for after 6 . . . BxP Black would be threatening . . . BxPch. White would therefore have to defend his King Bishop Pawn with an awkward move such as 7 Q–K2 or 7 Q–Q2–in either case badly blocking his development.

6 B–Q3?   . . .

The mistake we have previously seen. Now Black should play 6 . . . PxP!; 7 PxP, B–Q2! Instead, he carelessly transposes moves.

6 . . .   B–Q2?

Position after 6 . . . B–Q2?
White subtly exploits his opponent's error of judgment

Diagram 6

BLACK

WHITE

7 PxP!!   . . .

This surrender of the center comes as a great surprise to Black. The idea is to clear White's Queen 4 square for a piece. And later on, after . . . P–B3, the square King 5 becomes available for another White piece. In other words, White will be able to centralize pieces on his Queen 4 and King 5 squares. This is effectively brought out in the first Illustrative Game.

Before we go on to a study of the Normal Formations, it will be useful to compare the Pawn Skeletons of the two variations:

Normal Pawn Skeleton of the
Pawn-Chain Variation

Diagram 7a

BLACK

WHITE

In Diagram 7a we find that White's Queen 4 and King 5 squares are occupied by his Pawns. In Diagram 7b, however, White's Pawn-Chain has disappeared and these squares are available for occupation by centralized pieces. In Diagram 7a Black has the initiative through his pressure on the base of White's Pawn-Chain. In Diagram 7b White has the initiative by reason of his occupation of the center squares.

The following discussion of the Normal formations will emphasize the position of Pawns and pieces in the Pawn-Chain

Normal Pawn Skeleton of the
Centralization Variation

Diagram 7b

BLACK

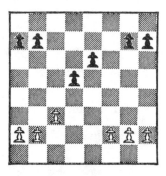

WHITE

Variation—with only occasional references to the Centralization Variation.

White's Normal Formation

White's *King Rook Pawn* generally remains unmoved.

White's *King Knight Pawn* advances one square so that White can play K–N2 (after K–B1) to carry out artificial castling.

White's *King Bishop Pawn* has the long-distance aim of menacing Black's Pawn-Chain by means of P–KB4–5. However, as we have seen from the discussion of the play from Diagram 3, White has to be very careful in his timing when he decides to advance his King Bishop Pawn.

White's *King Pawn* goes to King 4 on the first move and to King 5 on the third move. Its object is to try to cramp Black's game. A significant aspect of this is that the presence of White's

Pawn at King 5 prevents Black from posting his King Knight at its generally best square (Black's King Bishop 3).

Sometimes Black plays . . . P–KB3 and White's King Pawn captures. There will then be a clash of two concepts: does White get more benefit from occupying King 5 than Black gets from occupying the half-open King Bishop file? More on this point in the first Illustrative Game.

White's *Queen Pawn* plays to Queen 4 on the second move, and soon becomes the base of White's Pawn-Chain. In the Pawn-Chain Variation White will strive to keep a Pawn at Queen 4. In the Centralization Variation he will gladly exchange his Queen Pawn for Black's Queen Bishop Pawn (QPxQBP) because he wants to empty the center squares and occupy them with his centralized pieces.

White's *Queen Bishop Pawn* plays to Queen Bishop 3 to support the base of his Pawn-Chain at Queen 4.

White's *Queen Knight Pawn* generally advances one square in the Pawn-Chain Variation. The purpose is to fianchetto the White Queen Bishop to protect the base of White's Pawn-Chain at Queen 4. But P–QN4 may sometimes follow P–QR3.

In the Centralization Variation, White's Queen Knight Pawn may advance to Queen Knight 4 (as in the first Illustrative Game) after White has played QPxQBP and Black has replied . . . BxQBP. The purpose of P–QN4 in that event is to drive off Black's King Bishop from its important diagonal. However, the Queen Knight Pawn must not be pushed blindly. The advance of this Pawn must be part of a general attempt to control the black squares (Queen 4, King 5, perhaps Queen Bishop 5).

White's *Queen Rook Pawn* remains at Queen Rook 2 as a rule. However, in the Pawn-Chain Variation White often plays P–QR3 in order to drive away the Black King Bishop, and then continues P–QN4. Sometimes this is done in order to prepare to occupy Queen Bishop 5 with the White Queen Knight.

As for White's pieces:

White's *King Knight* plays to King Bishop 3 to support the base of White's Pawn-Chain in the Pawn-Chain Variation. However, in the Centralization Variation this Knight has good prospects of ending up at Queen 4 or King 5 if those squares are emptied by the removal of a Pawn.

White's *Queen Knight* always presents problems in the Pawn-Chain Variation, as the normal development N–QB3 or QN–Q2 would lead to the loss of White's Queen Pawn. The only remaining alternative seems N–QR3–QB2, which has the virtue of protecting the base of White's Pawn-Chain. However, this Knight development also has defects: it leaves the Knight in rather a passive situation and it interferes with White's hopes of using his Rooks effectively on the open Queen Bishop file.

White's *King Bishop* is best developed at King 2 in the Pawn-Chain Variation. Frequently B–Q3 is tried, but, as we saw in the discussion of Diagram 5, this only leads to loss of time when Black plays properly.

In the Centralization Variation, the most effective spot for this Bishop is Queen 3. This gives White genuine attacking chances, as we shall see in the first Illustrative Game.

White's *Queen Bishop* is something of a problem child in the Pawn-Chain Variation. The best use for it that White can devise is to play B–QN2 (after P–QN3). Here the Bishop has the useful function of defending the base of White's Pawn-Chain. But the Bishop suffers from the drawback of being hemmed in by White's Pawn-Chain, which is on black squares and thus reduces the Bishop's mobility appreciably.

White's *King Rook* also presents some problems in the Pawn-Chain Variation. This is due to White's loss of the castling privilege, which means there will be a delay in getting this Rook into active play. Sometimes this Rook can be brought to the Queen Bishop file when it is possible to double Rooks on that file. Or, if Black plays badly, the King Rook can go to King Bishop 1 to support the advance of White's King Bishop Pawn. It must be emphasized that this advance will be made possible only by poor play on Black's part. And even if this advance is possible, it will become available only in a fairly far advanced stage of the middle game.

White's *Queen Rook* has a natural post at Queen Bishop 1 on the open Queen Bishop file in the Pawn-Chain Variation.

White's *Queen* has trouble finding a good square in the Pawn-Chain Variation. This is explained by the necessity for having the Queen protect the base of White's Pawn-Chain. The fact that White's Queen has to be assigned this menial task speaks badly for the Pawn-Chain Variation from White's point of view. White should at least strive for Q–Q2, in order to establish the communication of White's Rooks as soon as possible.

White's *King* castles normally in the Centralization Variation. However, in the Pawn-Chain Variation, as we have seen, the King is likely to be in trouble. Forfeiting the castling privilege, the White King must go to King Bishop 1 and then King Knight 2 (after the preliminary P–KN3).

Black's Normal Formation

Black's *King Rook Pawn* sometimes goes to King Rook 4 in the Pawn-Chain Variation. The purpose of this is to prevent White from playing P–KN4 and driving away the Black Knight anchored at Black's King Bishop 4 square.

Black's *King Knight Pawn* should not be moved from its original square. As quite a few of the Black Pawns are on white squares, it follows that Black must be careful not to lose control of the black squares. In particular, . . . P–KN3 would seriously weaken Black's command of the black squares.

Black's *King Bishop Pawn* is often advanced one square in the

Pawn-Chain Variation. This advance has positive and negative features. It has the advantage of opening the King Bishop file and thus giving Black's game a more aggressive cast. On the other hand, it has the drawback of leaving Black with a backward King Pawn which White can attack along the half-open King file.

Another drawback, from Black's point of view, is that after White plays KPxKBP his King 5 square can be occupied by his powerfully centralized King Knight. Black can prevent this by answering KPxKBP with . . . NPxBP (instead of retaking with a piece on his King Bishop 3 square). This gives Black an open King Knight file, but at the cost of leaving his King in rather an exposed state. So, as you can see, . . . P–KB3 calls for a lot of reflection pro and con before Black can finally decide on its merits.

Black's *King Pawn* goes to King 3 on the first move. This, in combination with 2 . . . P–Q4, involves the possibility that Black's Queen Bishop will be shut in for a long time. It also may lead to situations in which Black is weak on the black squares because too many of his Pawns are on white squares and consequently do not command black squares.

Black's *Queen Pawn* advances to Queen 4 on the second move and immediately poses a crucial question to White: who shall control the center, and how? For some latent drawbacks of the Pawn-Chain see the remarks on Black's King Pawn.

Black's *Queen Bishop Pawn* always plays to Queen Bishop 4 at a very early stage to attack the base of White's Pawn-Chain. This is one of the basic ideas of the defense.

Because this advance has so much significance as a form of counterattack, it is bad play to advance the Queen Bishop Pawn another step to Queen Bishop 5. (This is a strategical mistake often committed by inexperienced players.)

The reason why . . . P–QB5? is bad is that it dissipates the tension in the center by relaxing the pressure against White's

Queen Pawn. Secondly, . . . P–QB5 creates a new Pawn-Chain with White's Queen Bishop Pawn as the base. The White Queen Bishop Pawn is solidly defended by its Queen Knight Pawn. The resulting stability of the center leaves White free to exploit his superior mobility. This will generally take the form of seeking a King-side attack.

There is still another drawback to . . . P–QB5? It puts another Black Pawn on a white square and thus contributes to the danger that Black may become very weak on the black squares.

Black's *Queen Knight Pawn* should remain on its original square. This leaves Black the option of playing . . . P–QN3 if necessary to drive off a White piece that has established itself on White's Queen Bishop square.

Black's *Queen Rook Pawn* often goes to Queen Rook 3 in positions where his King Bishop has been exchanged. The object of this Pawn advance is to prevent White from playing N–QN5–Q6, which would give the Knight an unassailable position in the heart of Black's camp.

As for Black's pieces:

Black's *King Knight* cannot go to its normal square King Bishop 3 because of the White Pawn at King 5. (This means that in some cases White may get a good attack because of the absence of this excellent defensive piece from its usual haunts.) In the Pawn-Chain Variation Black's King Knight takes a favorable post with . . . N–K2–KB4 attacking the base of White's Pawn-Chain.

In the Centralization Variation, on the other hand, the indicated procedure for Black's King Knight is . . . KN–K2–KN3. From King Knight 3 the Knight attacks White's King Pawn on King 5—the Pawn no longer is guarded by White's Queen Pawn, for White has played QPxQBP. And if White's King Pawn has also been exchanged—as so often happens in the Centralization Variation—then Black's King Knight plays a valuable role at

King Knight 3 in preventing White's occupation of his King 5 square with a strongly centralized Knight.

Black's *Queen Knight* generally plays to Queen Bishop 3 at a very early stage. From here it exerts direct pressure on White's Queen Pawn and indirect pressure on White's King Pawn on White's King 5 square.

Black's *King Bishop* plays to Queen Knight 5 with check in the Pawn-Chain Variation in order to deprive White of the castling privilege. Later on the Bishop will probably retreat to King 2.

In the Centralization Variation this Bishop is usually posted at Queen Bishop 4 as a result of recapturing on that square after White has played QPxQBP. The Bishop has a fine diagonal here, especially when backed up by the Black Queen at his Queen Knight 3 square.

Black's *Queen Bishop* can be seriously limited in scope in the hands of an inexperienced player. The great danger for this Bishop is that it will be sadly hemmed in by Black Pawns on white squares. (This applies particularly to the Black Pawns on King 3 and Queen 4.)

However, a knowledgeable player can find ways of putting this Bishop to good use. For example, the Bishop can be used for strictly defensive purposes, lending solidity to Black's position. Or it can be employed on the Queen-side to good effect—sometimes by way of . . . B–Q2–QN4–QB5. Finally, after . . . P–KB3 a future opens up for this Bishop, unexpectedly enough, on the King-side. This last comes about by the maneuver . . . B–Q2–K1 –KR4.

Black's *King Rook* will go to the Queen Bishop file—perhaps for doubling Rooks on that file—when the play is of a predominantly Queen-side character. In cases where Black opens the King Bishop file with . . . P–KB3, he will naturally want to keep his King Rook on the King Bishop file. In fact, he may end up by doubling his Rooks on that file.

Black's *Queen Rook* belongs on the Queen Bishop file, which is half-open or open all the way.

Black's *Queen* goes to Queen Knight 3—usually at an early stage—to take part in the attack on the base of White's Pawn-Chain.

Black's *King* goes to King Knight 1 as a part of castling. There are some very rare cases in which the King remains in the center.

ILLUSTRATIVE GAMES

GAME 1

(is a famous game in which 3 P–K5 was revived in modern master play)

Carlsbad, 1911

WHITE	BLACK
A. Nimzovich	G. Salve
1 P–K4	P–K3
2 P–Q4	P–Q4
3 P–K5	P–QB4
4 P–QB3	N–QB3
5 N–B3	Q–N3
6 B–Q3?	. . .

As we know from the earlier discussion, this move is a strategical blunder. The right way is 6 B–K2, etc.

6 . . .   B–Q2?

Black blunders in turn. He should have played 6 . . . PxP!; 7 PxP, B–Q2. See the discussion of Diagram 4.

7   PxP!!   . . .

This is the line we know as the Centralization Variation.

White plays to occupy the center squares effectively with his pieces.

$$7 \quad \ldots \quad BxP$$
$$8 \quad Castles \quad \ldots$$

If Black had had any inkling of his opponent's reply, he would have played 8 . . . P–QR4 in order to prevent the thrust of White's Queen Knight Pawn.

Position after 8 Castles
Black plays into his opponent's hands

Diagram 8

BLACK

WHITE

$$8 \quad \ldots \quad P–B3$$

Black gleefully imagines that he is breaking up White's center. Actually he is giving White's pieces an opportunity to centralize powerfully.

$$9 \quad P–QN4!! \quad B–K2$$
$$10 \quad B–KB4! \quad PxP$$
$$11 \quad NxP \quad NxN$$
$$12 \quad BxN \quad \ldots$$

The result of the "demolition" of White's center is that he

has a powerfully centralized Bishop on King 5. Black has an open King Bishop file, which is of no importance here. On the other hand, his backward King Pawn is a lasting liability.

12 . . .   N–B3

It will not do to play 12 . . . B–KB3 because of 13 Q–R5ch, P–N3; 14 BxPch!, PxB; 15 QxPch, K–K2; 16 BxBch, NxB; 17 Q–N7ch and White wins.

13   N–Q2   . . .

Better than the plausible 13 Q–B2, Castles (K)!; 14 BxN, RxB; 15 BxPch, K–R1; 16 B–Q3, P–K4! and Black has ample compensation for his Pawn: the half-open King Bishop file, better development, the two Bishops, and a strong Pawn center. *The pressure in the center must be maintained.*

13   . . .   Castles (K)
14   N–B3   B–Q3

The plausible try 14 . . . B–N4 fails because of 15 B–Q4!, Q–R3; 16 BxB, QxB; 17 N–N5, Q–B3; 18 R–K1 (or 18 Q–K2) winning the backward King Pawn.

(See Diagram 9)

Here 15 B–Q4 looks plausible, but Black has 15 . . . Q–B2; 16 Q–K2, N–N5!; 17 P–KR3, P–K4! and Black has freed himself.

15   Q–K2!   QR–B1
16   B–Q4   Q–B2
17   N–K5   B–K1
18   QR–K1   . . .

Notice how White systematically strengthens his control of the King 5 square.

18   . . .   BxN

Not very inviting, but Black is in danger of strangling. If 18 . . . N–Q2; 19 NxN, BxN; 20 Q–R5 and wins (20 . . . P–KN3; 21 BxNP or 20 . . . P–KR3; 21 BxNP!).

Position after 14 . . . B–Q3
White maintains the policy of restriction

Diagram 9

BLACK

WHITE

19	BxB	Q–B3
20	B–Q4	B–Q2
21	Q–B2	R–KB2

So as to answer 22 BxN with 22 . . . PxB. Instead, White brings a Rook into the attack.

| 22 | R–K3! | P–QN3 |
| 23 | R–N3 | . . . |

Threatening to win a Pawn by BxN, etc.

| 23 | . . . | K–R1 |
| 24 | BxRP! | . . . |

(*See Diagram 10*)

If Black plays 24 . . . NxB there follows 25 Q–N6!, K–N1; 26 BxKNP, N–B1; 27 Q–R6, N–R2; 28 B–B6 dis ch and White wins.

| 24 | . . . | P–K4! |

If now 25 BxKP, NxB and Black is safe.

Position after 24 BxRP!
Can Black capture the Bishop?

Diagram 10

BLACK

WHITE

25 B–N6!   R–K2

White must play very well hereabouts because Black's center
Pawns have at last become mobile.

26 R–K1!   Q–Q3

Black is praying for 27 R/N3–K3?, N–N5!; 28 R/K3–K2?,
PxB! (or 28 . . . P–K5!) and Black wins.

27 B–K3!   P–Q5

For a moment it seems that Black has worked up a creditable
counterattack, but White slips out neatly.

(See Diagram 11)

28 B–N5!   . . .

White threatens 29 Q–Q1! followed by 30 BxN and 31 Q–
R5ch.

28 . . .   RxP
29 RxR   PxR
30 QxP   K–N1

Position after 27 . . . P–Q5
How does White refute the counterattack?

Diagram 11

BLACK

WHITE

The situation has cleared. Black has nothing to show for his clear Pawn minus.

31	P–QR3	K–B1
32	B–R4!	B–K1

White is threatening B–N3. Black hopes for 33 BxB, RxB; 34 B–N3, N–Q2.

| 33 | B–B5! | . . . |

So that if 33 . . . N–Q2; 34 B–N3! and Black's King Pawn must fall.

| 33 | . . . | Q–Q5 |

He saves the Pawn, but only at the cost of simplifying Black's technical problems.

34	QxQ	PxQ
35	RxR	KxR
36	B–Q3	K–Q3
37	BxN!	. . .

Thus White obtains an outside passed Pawn.

37	. . .	PxB
38	K–B1	B–B3
39	P–KR4!	Resigns

A bit too soon perhaps, but with a Pawn ahead and an outside passed Pawn, White has an easy win. An outstanding example of centralizing and blockading strategy.

GAME 2

(in which Black plays with devilish energy to demolish White's Pawn center)

Match, 1920

WHITE	BLACK
A. Nimzovich	E. Bogolyubov
1 P–K4	P–K3
2 P–Q4	P–Q4
3 P–K5	P–QB4
4 N–KB3	N–QB3
5 P–B3	Q–N3
6 B–K2	. . .

White avoids the inferior 6 B–Q3? but the difference doesn't seem to do him much good.

6	. . .	PxP
7	PxP	KN–K2

With the familiar threat of . . . N–B4 directed against White's Queen Pawn.

(See Diagram 12)

8	N–B3	. . .

Instead of defending his Queen Pawn in the usual manner (P–QN3 followed by B–N2), White prepares to drive off the Black Queen. But he still loses the castling privilege.

Position after 7 . . . KN–K2
How does White propose to defend his Queen Pawn?

Diagram 12

BLACK

WHITE

| 8 | . . . | N–B4 |
| 9 | N–QR4 | B–N5ch |

Interposition is unsatisfactory: for example, if 10 B–Q2, Q–R4; 11 B–B3, P–QN4 and Black wins a Pawn.

10	K–B1	Q–Q1
11	P–QR3	B–K2
12	P–QN4	Castles
13	KR–N1	. . .

Beginning a deeply thought out and yet suicidal maneuver. White wants to drive off the advanced Black Knight with P–N4, but this idea is too ambitious. The more modest P–N3 followed by K–N2 would have been a more reasonable procedure.

| 13 | . . . | P–B3! |
| 14 | P–N4?! | . . . |

Expecting the attacked Knight to slink away. Instead, Black reacts with an unexpected sacrifice.

14	. . .	KNxP!
15	NxN	NxN
16	QxN	PxP

In return for his sacrificed piece Black has two Pawns, the initiative, and lasting attacking prospects. Of course, 17 QxKP? will not do because of 17 . . . B–B3.

| | 17 | Q–Q2 | P–QN3! |

An interesting move which keeps White's Knight out of Queen Bishop 5 and also opens up two diagonals for Black's Queen Bishop.

| | 18 | P–KN5 | P–Q5!! |

Position after 18 . . . P–Q5!!
Does 19 B–Q3 give White the initiative?

Diagram 13

BLACK

WHITE

If White plays 19 B–Q3 (to stop . . . P–K5), there follows 19 . . . Q–Q4; 20 Q–K2 (threatens B–K4), B–N2; 21 BxPch?!, KxB; 22 Q–R5ch, K–N1; 23 P–N6 (apparently White has a mating attack), B–R3ch!; 24 K–K1, Q–K5ch followed by 25 . . . Q–R5 and Black wins.

19 B–Q4   P–N4!

Sacrificing to gain valuable time.

20 BxNP   Q–Q4

21 Q–K2   P–K5

Black's Pawns steadily become more menacing. Even the exchange of Queens cannot save White, for example 22 Q–B4, P–K6; 23 QxQ, PxQ!; 24 B–B6 (if 24 R–R2, B–R6ch; 25 K–K1, QR–B1 and Black has a winning game), B–R6ch; 25 K–K2, PxP; 26 R–B1, P–Q6ch and wins.

With every move the Black Pawns become more menacing.

22 B–QB4   P–Q6!

Again giving White a chance to exchange Queens, which would still not be enough to save the game: 23 BxQ, PxQch; 24 KxP, PxB; 25 N–B5, BxN; 26 PxB, P–Q5!; 27 B–N2, B–R3ch; 28 K–K1, P–K6!; 29 PxP, PxP and White is helpless against the coming . . . P–K7.

Position after 22 . . . P–Q6!
White reels under the hammer blows

Diagram 14

BLACK

WHITE

                        23   Q–R2   Q–Q5

Naturally Black does not mind 24 BxPch, BxB; 25 QxDch,
K–R1; 26 Q–R2 because of 26 . . . P–Q7! with an easy win, as
White cannot reply 27 BxP.

Meanwhile Black is threatening 24 . . . P–K6, hence White's
next move.

                        24   R–N4   P–Q7!
                        25   QxP   QxBch
                        26   Q–K2   Q–N6

Black has regained the sacrificed piece without any slowdown
of his attacking energy.

                        27   N–B5   BxN
                        28   PxB   B–R3!
                             Resigns

Because after 29 QxB, Q–Q8ch; 30 K–N2, QxRch; 31 K–
B1, Q–Q8ch; 32 K–N2, Q–B6ch with a mating attack. Black's
energetic play has been a joy to follow.

                     Some useful pointers

For White:

1. In the Pawn-Chain Variation, get your King into safety
and avoid premature attacks.

2. Try to get your Queen Bishop into good play.

3. Don't lose time while developing your King Bishop.

4. Dispute the possession of the open Queen Bishop file.

5. In the Centralization Variation, play consistently for the
occupation or control of the King 5 and Queen 4 squares by your
pieces.

6. The proper square for your King Bishop is Queen 3, not
King 2.

7. Beware of opportunities to win a Pawn at the cost of relaxing your pressure in the center.

8. Don't underestimate Black's opportunities for counterattack via the King Bishop file.

For Black:

1. In the Pawn-Chain Variation, establish your pressure at once against the base of White's Pawn-Chain.

2. Never commit the strategical blunder of stabilizing the center with . . . P–QB5?

3. Don't neglect your Queen Bishop. It is often possible to get it into good play after . . . P–KB3 by means of . . . B–Q2–K1–KR4.

4. Be on your guard against coming into an endgame with your Queen Bishop opposed to a White Knight. With the Bishop hemmed in by Black Pawns on white squares, the black squares will be at the mercy of White's Knight.

Conclusions

The move 3 P–K5 leads to exceedingly critical play. On the whole, White's difficulties are much greater than Black's.

Black is much better off in the Pawn-Chain Variation than he is in the Centralization Variation. Therefore he should be on the lookout for a timely . . . QBPxQP.

Even in the Centralization Variation, Black gets a playable game if he postpones . . . P–KB3 until he has first played . . . KN–K2–N3. It is advisable for him to advance his development instead of aiming for . . . P–KB3 at a time when his development has not progressed very far.

Lesson 4

CARO-KANN DEFENSE

WHITE	BLACK
1 P–K4	P–QB3

The variation covered in the lesson starts with these moves:

WHITE	BLACK
1 P–K4	P–QB3
2 P–Q4	P–Q4
3 N–QB3	PxP
4 NxP	B–B4

The Normal Pawn Skeleton

Diagram 1

BLACK

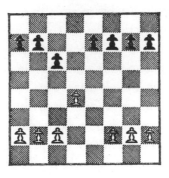

WHITE

Historical background

As we know, the French Defense (1 P–K4, P–K3) was popular all through the nineteenth century and even earlier. The Caro-Kann Defense, on the other hand, was classed among the "irregular defenses" until almost the beginning of the present century. Yet despite its comparatively recent entry into the ranks of the respectable openings, we do not know who invented it.

The defense is credited to Markus Kann and Horatio Caro, two players of mediocre rank. Their frequent adoption of this line attracted attention, however, and the defense eventually reached the height of its popularity in the 1920's and 1930's. It has appealed to such original thinkers as Nimzovich and Tartakover as well as to players with a solid and careful style (such as Capablanca, Flohr and Fine).

Theoretical background

While the Caro-Kann lacks the appeal nowadays that it used to have, it still ranks as one of the soundest defenses at Black's disposal. It has most of the virtues of the French Defense while generally being free of the latter's great drawback (imprisonment of Black's Queen Bishop).

In fact, it is a distinguishing mark of the Caro-Kann Defense that Black is almost invariably in a position to develop his Queen Bishop rapidly and effectively.

From this there follows a point of enormous importance: White's attacking chances are much less in the Caro-Kann than they are in the French. Here's why:

In the French Defense White often succeeds in posting his King Bishop on the splendid attacking diagonal Queen 3–King Rook 7. In the Caro-Kann, Black can generally forestall this aggressive setup with a timely . . . B–B4. (See Diagram 1, which makes this very clear.)

What have we learned about the Caro-Kann Defense so far?
We have learned that:
(1) Black gets an easy development.
(2) Black creates no weak points.
(3) White has difficulty in building up an attack.

Basic variations

To get a clear picture of this opening, let us study the main
line and some likely alternatives.

WHITE	BLACK
1 P–K4	P–QB3
2 P–Q4	. . .

The most obvious reply, although since 1930 the alternative
2 N–QB3, P–Q4; 3 N–B3 has greatly increased in popularity.
The purpose of 2 N–QB3 is to enable White to avoid commit-
ting himself in the center. The drawback to such a policy is that
Black, left to his own devices, has plenty of time and space to
further his own plans. On the other hand, if Black plays carelessly, he may find the resulting complications very bothersome.

2	. . .	P–Q4
3	N–QB3	. . .

From this move stems the variation to be studied in this lesson.

| 3 | . . . | PxP |

This is the only move worth considering.

If for example 3 . . . N–B3?; 4 P–K5!, KN–Q2; 5 B–Q3
(threatening 6 P–K6!, PxP; 7 Q–R5ch, P–KN3; 8 QxNPch!,
PxQ; 9 BxP mate!) and White has a notable plus in space and
mobility.

| 4 NxP | B–B4 |

Black develops his Bishop very early, and with gain of time,
to boot.

The alternative was 4 . . . N–B3, when 5 NxNch in reply

leaves Black with a disadvantageous doubled Pawn whichever way he recaptures.

The Basic Position (after 4 . . . B–B4)

Diagram 2

BLACK

WHITE

5   N–N3   . . .

The customary move. It has the drawback of leaving the Knight *decentralized* and therefore rather out of play.

For that reason some authorities have recommended 5 B–Q3!? with a view to sacrificing a Pawn in order to keep the Knight in the center and to gain time for development.

However, with cautious play Black should escape with a whole skin. A plausible sequence would be 5 . . . QxP; 6 N–KB3, Q–Q1; 7 Q–K2, BxN!; 8 BxB, N–B3; 9 B–Q3, QN–Q2; 10 Castles, P–K3. While White's game is more comfortable, he certainly does not have enough compensation for the sacrificed Pawn.

5   . . .   B–N3

White now has four main systems of development:

(a) 6 N–B3 followed by B–Q3 (or B–QB4) and eventually castling on the King-side.

(b) 6 P–KR4 (inducing . . . P–KR3 as a retreat for the Bishop) followed by the above moves and eventually castling Queen-side.

(c) 6 P–KB4, in which case White hopes to establish a strong point for one of his Knights at King 5—or else to obtain an attack along the King Bishop file by P–B5.

(d) 6 P–KR4 followed by N–R3–B4. This allows Black to get an excellent game with an early . . . P–K4.

The proper placement of the Pawns and pieces will be discussed in the two following sections.

White's Normal Formation

White's *King Rook Pawn* is sometimes advanced to King Rook 4. The idea is to provoke . . . P–KR3, forcing Black to exchange Bishops in reply to White's B–Q3. White recaptures with his Queen and is soon ready to castle Queen-side. This occurs in Illustrative Game 1.

White's *King Knight Pawn* remains on its original square.

White's *King Bishop Pawn* generally remains unmoved, except in Variation (c) in the previous note to White's fifth move.

This advance of White's King Bishop Pawn may involve drawbacks. It loosens his grip on certain center squares; and it may weaken him on the diagonal King Knight 1 to Queen Rook 7.

White's *King Pawn* disappears on Black's third move, being captured by Black's Queen Pawn.

White's *Queen Pawn* plays an important role: it controls the vital center square King 5, and in consequence often has the task of guarding an "outpost" Knight on the King 5 square. More likely than not, however, White's Queen Pawn disappears somewhere along the line after Black plays . . . P–QB4 and a Pawn exchange ensues. See Game 1 on this point.

White's *Queen Bishop Pawn* has a choice of moves. As long as his Queen Pawn remains on the board, it may seem advisable to give it extra support with P–QB3. After P–QB4, on the other hand, the Queen Pawn might turn out to be weak because it has been deprived of Pawn support. But perhaps this theorizing goes too far; if White has a sound position and a good development—as he generally has in the Caro-Kann—he can play P–QB4 without courting trouble.

*The Normal Pawn Skeleton after White
has played P–QB4*

Diagram 3a

BLACK

WHITE

(See Diagram 3b)

Suppose White's Queen Pawn is exchanged for Black's Queen Bishop Pawn (as mentioned in the discussion of White's Queen Pawn). In that case there is no objection to White's playing P–QB4. Keep these points in mind about the advance:

(a) After White's P–QB4, Black is prevented from posting any of his forces on his Queen 4 square—a key central square.

*The Normal Pawn Skeleton after Black
has replied . . . P–QB4 and a Pawn exchange has ensued, resulting in a Queen-
side majority of Pawns for White*

Diagram 3b

BLACK

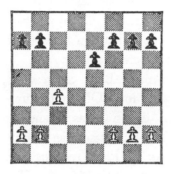

WHITE

(b) In situations where Black's Queen Bishop Pawn has
been exchanged for White's Queen Pawn, White has a Queen-
side majority of Pawns—three White Pawns against two Black
Pawns. The steady advance of the White Pawn majority should
eventually result in a passed Pawn for White. The point of all
this is that P–QB4 sets White's Pawn majority in motion.
Properly timed, the advance of this Queen-side Pawn majority
can constitute an important endgame advantage. This is due
to the relative remoteness of the resulting passed White Pawn
from both Kings.

Having played P–QB4, White must be careful about not
advancing P–B5 prematurely; for this at once gives Black's pieces
access to his coveted Queen 4 square.

Note, in addition, that P–B5 may leave White with an endgame weakness. After the customary exchange of Bishops in the

opening, White is left with a black-squared Bishop. The more White Pawns that are placed on black squares, the more mobility they take away from this Bishop. Thus P–B5 may aggravate this defect in White's position.

It is true that P–B5 often looks inviting, precisely because it sets White's Queen-side Pawn majority in motion. But this advance is most advantageous in the endgame, after a fair amount of simplification has taken place. During the middle game, with plenty of pieces still on the board, you can hardly expect your opponent to look on blandly while you advance a passed Pawn to the queening square.

And bear this in mind—Black can react aggressively to P–B5 with . . . P–QN3, or to P–QN4 (the supporting move) with . . . P–QR4. Then, if White has advanced prematurely on the Queen-side, Black's counterattack can be quite effective.

White's *Queen Knight Pawn* remains unmoved, except when it is played to Queen Knight 3 to support White's Queen Bishop Pawn after P–QB4; or when the Queen Knight Pawn advances to Queen Knight 4 after its neighbor Pawn has advanced to Queen Bishop 5. The precaution previously mentioned still applies; unless the advance P–QN4 is properly prepared, Black can react powerfully with . . . P–QR4.

White's *Queen Knight Pawn* remains unmoved, except in the case of an effective, well-timed general advance of the Queen-side Pawns.

As for White's pieces:

White's *King Knight,* as we have seen, generally goes to King Bishop 3 in order to control—in some cases occupy—the important center square King 5. There are times when the Knight is developed to King Bishop 4 via King Rook 3 or King 2; but this loses time, is not particularly effective and allows Black to counter energetically with . . . P–K4. (All this is borne out in Game 2.)

White's *Queen Knight* plays to Queen Bishop 3 on the third

move, arrives at King 4 on the fourth move, and then retreats to King Knight 3 when attacked by the Black Queen Bishop. At King Knight 3 this Knight is somewhat out of play, and in the middle game White will generally strive to get the Knight back to King 4 to enable it to play a valuable role in the center, or perhaps to exchange it (Game 1).

White's *King Bishop* is generally developed to Queen 3 and exchanged for Black's Queen Bishop (Game 1). Sometimes White develops this Bishop to Queen Bishop 4, but this seems rather pointless; its diagonal is broken there by the Black Pawn at King 3, and in addition the Bishop at Queen Bishop 4 hampers White if he wants to play P–QB4.

White's *Queen Bishop* generally does not come out until the ninth move or so (Game 1). By developing, it prepares for White's Queen-side castling. Later on, especially after the disappearance of White's Queen Pawn, this Bishop can take up a good post at Queen Bishop 3 (Game 1).

White's *King Rook* generally goes to King 1. On this half-open file it can support an outpost at King 5.

White's *Queen Rook* plays to Queen 1. (In the event of White's Queen-side castling, his Rook arrives at the desired square automatically.) Here the Rook protects White's Queen Pawn; or, in the event that the Queen Pawn disappears, the Rook can dispute control of the resulting open Queen file.

White's *Queen* is generally found at Queen 3 after the exchange of Bishops (Game 1). But frequently the Queen will later retreat to King 2, to avoid any Black counteraction with one of his Rooks on the Queen file.

Note: White may sometimes castle King-side, especially if he has omitted P–KR4. But Queen-side castling is preferred in modern play, with the White King often continuing to Queen Knight 1 (Game 1). Here the King guards White's Queen Rook Pawn; gets into safety so as not to be somewhat exposed after

P–QB4; and, as seen in the above game, avoids an exchange of Bishops which would ease Black's game.

Black's Normal Formation

Black's *King Rook Pawn* is advanced one square to King Rook 3 whenever Black's Queen Bishop is menaced by White's P–KR4. It is poor policy to answer P–KR4 with . . . P–KR4, however; for in that case White's maneuver N–KR3–B4 can be very inconvenient for Black.

In the event that Black allows the capture of his Queen Bishop at his King Knight 3 square, this is advisable only when Black's King Rook Pawn is still at King Rook 2 to do the recapturing.

Black's *King Knight Pawn* and *King Bishop Pawn* remain on their original squares.

Black's *King Pawn* advances one square as a rule. However, in those variations in which White's King Knight does not go to his King Bishop 3, it often becomes feasible for Black to play . . . P–K4.

Black's *Queen Pawn* disappears in the exchange on the third move.

Black's *Queen Bishop Pawn* advances one square on his first move. At a later stage, Black can gain some freedom by moving the Pawn up another square (. . . P–QB4). Nevertheless, this second advance calls for accurate timing; otherwise Black may find that he has opened up the position for White's pieces or else that White's resulting Queen-side Pawn majority has become too menacing.

Black's *Queen Knight Pawn* generally remains unmoved, except that . . . P–QN3 may turn out to be useful in restraining the advance of White's Queen-side majority, or in breaking it up once it has advanced.

Black's *Queen Rook Pawn* is even less likely to move, except in situations where White has played P–QN4. In that event, . . . P–QR4 is an effective counter.

As for Black's pieces:

Black's *King Knight* is almost always played to King Bishop 3. There is an important exception—when White plays an early P–KB4. In that case, the development . . . N–K2 serves a useful purpose in counteracting the further advance of White's King Bishop Pawn. (Of course, in such cases . . . N–K2 should be preceded by . . . B–Q3.)

Black's *Queen Knight* plays to Queen 2, where it has the important function of bearing on the vital King 4 and Queen Bishop 4 squares in Black's camp. An important point: whenever White is ready to play N–K5, Black should forestall him by immediately playing . . . N–Q2.

Black's *King Bishop* is played to King 2 as a rule, in keeping with the predominantly conservative character of Black's setup. However, there are some situations where . . . B–Q3 has a point in its favor. For example, . . . B–Q3 can be played to prevent White's N–K5—or to undermine White's Knight if it is already posted on that square. Still another purpose of . . . B–Q3 is to continue with . . . B–B5 in some situations to bring about an exchange of Bishops, a theme illustrated in Game 1.

There is another way in which Black's King Bishop can find an effective post. Suppose a White Knight goes to King 5 and is exchanged there. White's Queen Pawn recaptures. In that event, the excellent development . . . B–QB4 is available for Black's King Bishop.

Black's *Queen Bishop* plays effectively to King Bishop 4 on the fourth move. The Bishop is so well placed here, in fact, that White almost invariably plays B–Q3 to exchange off Black's well-posted Bishop.

Black's *Rooks* generally play to King 1 and Queen 1. In that case Black's King Rook is handy against surprise attacks on the King file, while his Queen Rook exerts pressure on White's Queen Pawn. Alternative setups: Black King Rook at King Bishop 1 and Queen Rook at Queen 1 (especially after King-side castling); or Black King Rook at King Rook 1 and Queen Rook at Queen 1 (after Queen-side castling).

Black's *Queen* almost invariably gets posted at Queen Bishop 2, observing the vital King 4 square, generally preparing for Queen-side castling and in any event assuring communication between Black's Rooks.

Note: Queen-side castling is the rule rather than the exception for Black. In that case the advance . . . P–QB4 is not undertaken lightly, as it may leave the Black King somewhat exposed to attack. But if Black castles King-side, he need have no worries on this score.

ILLUSTRATIVE GAMES

GAME 1

(shows what happens when both sides strive for the Normal Formation)

New York, 1939

	WHITE R. *Fine*	BLACK M. *Hanauer*
1	P–K4	P–QB3
2	P–Q4	P–Q4
3	N–QB3	PxP
4	NxP	B–B4
5	N–N3	B–N3
6	P–KR4	P–KR3

Black creates a retreat for his Bishop in the event of P–R5.

7 N–B3   . . .

If Black answers this move carelessly he gets into trouble, for example 7 . . . P–K3; 8 N–K5, B–R2; 9 Q–R5 (threatening mate!) with a strong initiative for White. But as Black plays, he is safe enough.

Position after 7 N–B3
Black must be on his guard against N–K5

Diagram 4

BLACK

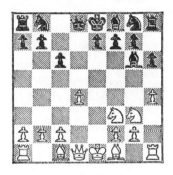

WHITE

7 . . .   N–Q2

This takes care of White's threatened N–K5.

8 B–Q3   BxB

Black has little choice, as the exchange of Bishops after 8 . . . B–N3? would leave him with a shattered Pawn position.

9 QxB   KN–B3

10 B–Q2   . . .

White prepares for Queen-side castling.

10 . . .   P–K3

11 Castles (Q)   Q–B2

Black is also castling on the Queen's wing.

12   K–N1   Castles

Position after 12 . . . Castles
White's K–N1 is an important part of his system

Diagram 5

BLACK

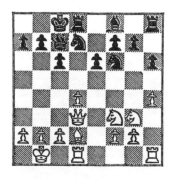

WHITE

Both sides have made considerable progress in achieving their Normal Formations. White's last move looks a bit mysterious, but its subtle meaning will become clear on move 15. As for Black, he must strive for freedom, and an early . . . P–B4 is quite safe here.

13   P–B4   B–Q3

Not the best. The most accurate procedure was 13 . . . P–B4; 14 B–B3, PxP; 15 BxP, B–B4 getting the Bishop to Queen Bishop 4 in one move. In that case the game would be almost level with White having a slight pull, thanks to his somewhat greater mobility.

14   N–K4   NxN
15   QxN   P–QB4

The alternative 15 . . . N–B3; 16 Q–K2, B–B5 does not

ease Black's game because White evades the exchange by 17 B–B3! (this was the point of White's 12 K–N1).

16 B–B3 N–B3

17 Q–K2 . . .

If now 17 . . . PxP; 18 BxP, B–B4 and it turns out that Black has taken two moves to get his Bishop to Queen Bishop 4. This loss of time is by no means a trifling matter, for after 19 BxB, QxB; 20 N–K5, Q–B2; 21 P–B5! Black is under pressure (he cannot play 21 . . . QxP because of 22 R–QB1).

17 . . . P–R3

A waiting move.

18 N–K5 BxN

This has a point, as it opens the Queen file, leading to possibilities of exchanging all the Rooks. In any event Black has nothing better.

19 PxB N–Q2

20 R–Q6 N–N1

21 KR–Q1 N–B3

Not 21 . . . RxR? for then 22 PxR wins Black's King Knight Pawn. This explains his next move.

22 P–R5 KR–N1

Now he is ready for . . . RxR.

23 Q–K3! . . .

Attacking Black's Queen Bishop Pawn. His situation is now very difficult, for example 23 . . . P–QN3; 24 Q–B3, RxR; 25 RxR, N–N1 (25 . . . K–N2? loses to 26 RxN!, QxR; 27 QxPch, etc.); 26 Q–K4 (threatens Q–R7, etc.), P–N3; 27 B–Q2! and it is very questionable whether Black can hold together his precarious position.

(See Diagram 6)

A gallant try. Black figures that since he is very likely lost after quiet continuations he might as well plunge into complications.

Position after 23 Q–K3!
The pressure on Black's game has become well-nigh unbearable

Diagram 6

BLACK

WHITE

23	. . .	N–Q5!?
24	RxRch	RxR
25	BxN	. . .

White calmly falls in with his opponent's plans, satisfied that he can win the ending resulting from 25 . . . Q–Q2; 26 Q–KN3, PxB; 27 QxP, P–Q6; 28 QxRP, etc.

Nor does White flinch from 25 . . . Q–N3 with the plausible continuation 26 BxP!, RxRch; 27 K–B2, Q–Q1 (forced); 28 B–N6, Q–Q2 (again forced); 29 Q–B5ch and White wins the Rook!

25	. . .	PxB
26	RxP	RxR
27	QxR	Q–R4
28	P–KN4!	Q–K8ch
29	K–B2	Q–K7ch
30	K–N3	. . .

By means of his Queen checks Black is able to menace a

whole flock of White Pawns. If he thinks that this will hamper the White pieces' freedom of action, he is at once taught the error of his ways. For White conceives a daring plan to threaten mate by bringing his King to Queen Knight 6 and thereby threatening mate in due course. Black is able to avoid this grim possibility at the cost of allowing the exchange of Queens with an easily won King and Pawn ending for White.

Position after 30 K–N3
White's King is headed for Queen Knight 6!

Diagram 7

BLACK

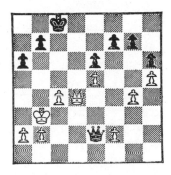

WHITE

30	...	K–N1
31	K–N4	Q–K8ch
32	K–R4	Q–K7
33	K–R5	Q–B6

In order to answer 34 K–N6 with 34 . . . Q–QB3ch.

34	Q–B5!	Q–K7
35	P–QN4	Q–Q6

Black hopes for a last swindle: on 36 K–N6?? he forces mate with 36 . . . Q–Q1ch, etc.

36	Q–Q6ch	QxQ
37	PxQ	P–KN3
38	K–N6	. . .

Threatening 39 P–Q7 followed by promotion and mate.

38	. . .	K–B1
39	P–B5!	PxP
40	PxP	P–K4
41	P–Q7ch	Resigns

For if 41 . . . KxP; 42 KxP and White's supported, passed
Queen Bishop Pawn marches to the queening square. Triumph
of White's Queen-side Pawn majority.

GAME 2

(illustrates how Black seizes the initiative when White adopts
an inferior line of play)

Lodz, 1935

WHITE	BLACK
L. Steiner	*K. Opocensky*
1 P–K4	P–QB3
2 P–Q4	P–Q4
3 N–QB3	PxP
4 NxP	B–B4
5 N–N3	B–N3
6 N–R3	. . .

(See Diagram 8)

White has branched off from the standard 6 N–B3 continuation. He intends N–B4 followed by NxB, thereby obtaining
the theoretical advantage of two Bishops against Bishop and
Knight. But this time-consuming maneuver allows Black to get
a big lead in development.

Position after 6 N–R3
White is wasting too much time with his Knight moves

Diagram 8

BLACK

WHITE

6	. . .	N–Q2
7	N–B4	P–K4!

The direct consequence of the White Knight's failure to occupy King Bishop 3.

8	NxB	RPxN
9	PxP	Q–R5!

The measly 9 . . . NxP, allowing the exchange of Queens, naturally does not appeal to White.

White can play to hold his extra Pawn with 10 P–KB4; but after 10 . . . Castles (threatening . . . NxP); 11 B–Q2, N–R3 (threatening . . . N–KB4) Black has a tremendous initiative.

10	P–K6	. . .

White returns the Pawn, but his position remains uncomfortable.

10	. . .	PxP
11	Q–K2	Castles

Black makes no attempt to guard his King Pawn, for if 12 QxP, KN–B3 (threatening to win White's Queen); 13 B–K2, B–N5ch followed by . . . KR–K1 and Black has a terrific lead in development.

          12   B–Q2   . . .

White gets ready to castle—his only practical chance to escape disaster.

          12   . . .   KN–B3
          13   Castles   B–B4!

Position after 13 . . . B–B4!
White has been left far behind in development

Diagram 9

BLACK

WHITE

          14   B–K3?   . . .

This plausible move loses quickly. His only chance was 14 P–KB3.

          14   . . .   N–N5!
          15   BxB   NxB

Black threatens immediate destruction with 16 . . . Q–N4ch; 17 K–N1, RxRch; 18 QxR, NxBP, etc.

16 P–QB3   Q–N4ch

This wins even more rapidly than 16 . . . RxRch; 17 KvR, R–Qich; 18 K–B2, NxBP—which is also good enough, for if 19 QxN, Q–R5ch and Black forces mate.

17 K–B2   RxR
18 KxR   R–B1!

Decisive, for if 19 P–B3, R–Qich; 20 K–B2, N–K6ch; 21 K–N1, R–Q8ch winning White's Queen.

19 P–KB4   RxP
20 K–K1   R–B7
21 Q–Q1   Q–K6ch
22 B–K2   . . .

Position after 22 B–K2
Black is set for the kill

Diagram 10

BLACK

WHITE

22 . . .   RxBch
Resigns

For if 23 QxR, N–Q6ch; 24 K–Q1, Q–B8 mate; or 23 NxR, N–Q6ch and White must give up his Queen.

Some useful pointers

For White:

1. Play to control the important King 5 square.
2. After Black plays . . . P–QB4, look for a favorable opportunity to establish a Queen-side majority of Pawns.
3. Play your own Queen Bishop Pawn to Queen Bishop 4 when feasible. In this way you stop Black's pieces from occupying his Queen 4 square.
4. Once you have played P–QB4, don't be in a hurry to continue P–B5—for in that case Black will be able to plant a piece at his Queen 4 square after all.

For Black:

1. Try to occupy your Queen 4 square—or at any rate to control it.
2. Strive to free your game by . . . P–QB4—but not at a point where you actually give White's pieces greater freedom of action.
3. Bring one of your Rooks to the Queen file, so that you can dispute control of the file after . . . P–QB4.
4. Take the sting out of a possible N–K5 on White's part. Do this by a timely development of your Queen Knight (. . . N–Q2).
5. Generally speaking, you ought to avoid the doubling of your King Knight Pawn which arises from the exchange of your Bishop on your King Knight 3 square.

Conclusions

The Caro-Kann Defense—and especially the variation studied here—gives Black a sound but rather stodgy game. For that reason you should play it against an opponent whom you find really formidable.

Players who are enterprising will naturally prefer to use defenses which are more lively if more risky too.

The player of the Black pieces must also remember that complications are not automatically ruled out. If White is an aggressive player he may seek tactical complications that may turn the game far away from the quiet paths sought by the defender.

Lesson 5

ALEKHINE'S DEFENSE

(Four Pawns' Game)

WHITE	BLACK
1 P–K4	N–KB3

Black's astounding move relies on shock value to rock White back on his heels.

Position after 1 . . . N–KB3
White must choose between an
aggressive or noncommittal course

Diagram 1

BLACK

WHITE

Of course White can answer Black's provocative move with some perfectly safe reply such as 2 N–QB3 or even 2 P–Q3. But it goes against the grain to respond passively. A more likely continuation is the following:

2	P–K5	N–Q4
3	P–QB4	N–N3
4	P–Q4	P–Q3
5	P–B4	. . .

This line of play is sometimes known as the "Four Pawns' Game" because White has advanced four of his Pawns.

5	. . .	PxP
6	BPxP	. . .

Position after 6 BPxP
Are White's advanced Pawns strong or weak?

Diagram 2

BLACK

WHITE

Two schools of thought

Considerable argument has raged over the question, Are White's advanced Pawns strong or weak? Those who favor Black point out triumphantly that he has achieved what he wanted—he has lured the White Pawns on, and will later on be able to exploit that weakness (assuming that it exists).

The other side holds that Black has paid a heavy price by having his King Knight driven to a square which is equivalent to exile. At Queen Knight 3 the Knight is rather out of play. Black will have to spend valuable time getting this piece into the game.

But the defenders of Black's side of the argument point out that the position of the Knight is not basic because the Knight *can* move to a better square. What matters, they say, is that White's Queen Pawn is a *permanent* target for the Black pieces.

The Normal Pawn Skeleton

Diagram 3

BLACK

WHITE

A glance at Diagram 3 shows that there is some merit in this argument. Thanks to the advance of its neighboring Pawns, White's Queen Pawn certainly cannot depend on Pawn protection. Hence it will have to be protected by pieces. There is also the possibility that Black can play . . . P–QB4 at some time, liquidating White's Queen Pawn and in effect leaving White's King Pawn high and dry.

All this sounds very cogent. How is White to meet these potential dangers? The answer is that he must stress rapid, effective development. Only by striving for a smart initiative can he neutralize the theoretical drawbacks of his position.

If this sounds desperate, it isn't meant to be. The following discussion will show that White's position, properly developed, is rich in resources.

The normal course of the variation

	WHITE	BLACK
1	P–K4	N–KB3
2	P–K5	N–Q4
3	P–QB4	N–N3
4	P–Q4	. . .

The usual move is now 4 . . . P–Q3, but if Black wants to continue being provocative, he can play 4 . . . N–B3? But this is too much of a good thing, and in fact it loses a piece. White replies 5 P–Q5! with these possibilities:

1. 5 . . . NxKP; 6 P–B5, N/N3–B5; 7 P–B4.
2. 5 . . . N–N1; 6 P–B5.
3. 5 . . . N–N5; 6 P–B5, N/N3xP; 7 P–QR3.

In every case White wins a piece. This is important because it demonstrates the dynamic punch of White's formation.

(See Diagram 4)

4	. . .	P–Q3
5	P–B4	. . .

Position after 4 P–Q4
Black must proceed discreetly

Diagram 4

BLACK

WHITE

More aggressive than 5 KPxP, which commits White much less but also gives him diminished prospects.

     5 . . .   PxP
     6 BPxP   N–QB3

Now this developing move is in order, as P–Q5 would simply lose a Pawn.

     7 B–K3   B–B4

Note that Black is actually ahead in development, with three pieces developed to White's two. But mere counting does not tell the story. As we know, Black's decentralized Knight at Queen Knight 3 does not play a very useful role.

     8 N–QB3   P–K3
     9 B–K2   . . .

Here is where Black must choose between three sharply differentiated lines of play.

    1. 9 . . . B–K2 followed by castling King-side. This is the line of play that appears in the second Illustrative Game.

2. 9 . . . N–N5 followed by 10 . . . P–QB4–an attempt
to break up White's central Pawn formation. This is the line of
play featured in the first Illustrative Game.

3. 9 . . . Q–Q2 followed by . . . Castles. As this variation is
not supported by an Illustrative Game, we shall give it some
passing study here.

Position after 9 B–K2
Which defense shall Black choose?

Diagram 5

BLACK

WHITE

Diagram 5 will be our point of departure for examining the
Normal Formation for both sides. But first we want to see the
consequences of 9 . . . Q–Q2.

     9 . . .   Q–Q2
   10 N–B3   Castles

The purpose of Black's castling on the Queen-side is to bring
pressure to bear on White's Queen Pawn. But White remains
unruffled.

   11 Castles   P–B3

An attempt to break up White's Pawn center. An even more dangerous-looking menace to White's center would be 11 . . . B–KN5 threatening to win the Queen Pawn by removing White's King Knight. The consequences might be: 12 P–QR4!, BxN (See Diagram 6); 13 PxB!, NxQP; 14 P–R5, N–R1 (the miserable position of this Knight is a great plus for White); 15 P–R6!, P–QN3 (Black cannot allow White to open the Queen Rook file); 16 BxN!, QxBch; 17 QxQ, RxQ; 18 N–N5 and White regains his Pawn advantageously.

> 12　P–Q5!　　. . .

Again White resorts to a promising Pawn sacrifice to seize a strong initiative.

12	. . .	NxKP
13	NxN	PxN
14	P–QR4!	K–N1
15	Q–N3	B–N3
16	QR–Q1	. . .

White's aggressive position is well worth a Pawn. These spirited variations give us a good insight into the lively style of play which is called for in this opening.

White's Normal Formation

White's *King Rook Pawn* and *King Knight Pawn* remain on their original squares.

White's *King Bishop Pawn* advances to King Bishop 4 early in the opening to support his King Pawn. When Black plays . . . QPxKP, White replies KBPxKP with a highly aggressive though possibly vulnerable position in the center.

White's *King Pawn* advances to K5 attacking Black's King Knight on the second move. After the exchanges in the center, White's King Pawn is replaced by his King Bishop Pawn. Whether this advanced Pawn is strong or weak—that is the question.

White's *Queen Pawn* plays to Queen 4 in the opening. This Pawn is the prime target of Black's pressure and White should concentrate on protecting it efficiently or finding ample compensation for its loss. When Black plays . . . P–QB4, this will be followed by . . . QBPxQP bringing White's King Knight into more efficient play.

White's *Queen Bishop Pawn* plays to Queen Bishop 4 early in the opening to drive Black's King Knight away from its centralized post.

It is almost invariably a strategical mistake, by the way, to play P–QB5, as this gives Black's King Knight a splendidly centralized post at Black's Queen 4 square.

White's *Queen Knight Pawn* and *Queen Rook Pawn* generally remain unmoved. They may sometimes advance as part of a general offensive on the Queen-side after Black has played . . . P–QB4 followed by . . . QBPxQP. (This exchange gives White a Queen-side majority of Pawns, which explains why the Pawns are likely to advance in such cases.)

White's Queen Rook Pawn will sometimes advance to Queen Rook 3 to drive away Black's Queen Knight which has played to Queen Knight 5.

As for White's pieces:

White's *King Knight* plays to King Bishop 3. A useful precaution: postpone the development of this Knight so as to stave off . . . B–KN5 in reply which could constitute a menace to White's Queen Pawn.

White's *Queen Knight* plays to Queen Bishop 3, in some cases supporting the violent thrust P–Q5. Where this advance can be carried out successfully it will disorganize Black's game.

White's *King Bishop* plays to King 2—not to Queen 3. A prime example of the difficulties connected with B–Q3 can be seen in the following example: 1 P–K4, N–KB3; 2 P–K5, N–Q4; 3 P–QB4, N–N3; 4 P–Q4, P–Q3; 5 P–B4, PxP; 6 BPxP,

N–B3; 7 B–K3, B–B4; 8 B–Q3?, BxB; 9 QxB, NxKP! and Black has a winning game.

Another argument against playing B–Q3 is that it blocks White's defense of his Queen Pawn along the Queen file and also exposes him to a possible pin on his King Knight by . . . B–KN5.

Note that in cases where Black has played . . . B–KN5 and continues with . . . BxN after B–K2, White will be unable to recapture with his King Bishop because that piece also has the task of guarding White's Queen Bishop Pawn against capture by Black's Knight on Queen Knight 3. This is illustrated in the characteristic position shown in Diagram 6.

Black has just played . . . BxN

Diagram 6

BLACK

WHITE

You may recognize this position as one that turned up in the discussion of Diagram 5. White has three possible ways of recapturing, but one of them obviously will not do: BxB? would be answered by . . . NxBP breaking up White's position.

White's *Queen Bishop* plays a defensive but vital role in guarding his Queen Pawn. In positions where White plays P–Q5 or where his Queen Pawn is exchanged for Black's Queen Bishop Pawn, attractive vistas open up for the Queen Bishop, as it can take an aggressive role in that case.

White's *King Rook* will generally remain on King Bishop 1 after castling. There are occasional opportunities for attack or counterplay along the half-open King Bishop file.

White's *Queen Rook* is likely to go to Queen 1 to assist in the protection of his Queen Pawn. In situations where Black castles Queen-side, White's Queen Rook may remain on its original square to support the forward thrust of his Queen Rook Pawn to good effect.

White's *Queen* may play to Queen 2 to allow further protection for the Queen Pawn if needed. When Black castles Queen-side White's Queen is aggressively posted at Queen Knight 3.

When Black castles King-side White may play Q–K1, making room for the White Queen Rook at Queen 1. This avoids dangerous pinning attacks from a Black Rook on the same file. Q–K1 also has the virtue of possibly preparing for a King-side attack by Q–N3.

White's *King* plays to King Knight 1 by castling.

Black's Normal Formation

Black's *King Rook Pawn* remains at King Rook 2.

Black's *King Knight Pawn* likewise remains on its original square, except in rare cases when Black fianchettoes his King Bishop to menace White's advanced King Pawn with the threat of . . . P–QB4.

Black's *King Bishop Pawn* is generally played to King Bishop 3 in the early middle game in order to undermine White's center. However, after White replies KPxKBP it turns out that Black is left with Pawn weaknesses too.

Black's *King Pawn* plays to King 3 in order to permit the development of Black's King Bishop.

Black's *Queen Pawn* advances to Queen 3, opening the diagonal of Black's Queen Bishop and also preparing the exchange . . . QPxKP.

Black's *Queen Bishop Pawn* often advances to Queen Bishop 4 in situations where Black castles King-side. The intention here is to shatter White's Pawn center. In games in which Black castles on the Queen-side, Black's Queen Bishop Pawn remains at home. Its advance would only render the Black King's situation insecure.

Black's *Queen Knight Pawn* and *Queen Rook Pawn* generally remain on their original squares.

Black's *King Knight*, as we know, is boldly played to King Bishop 3 on the first move, and is thereupon driven to Black's Queen Knight 3 square. As a rule a Knight is badly placed on this square. In this case Black has some compensation in the Knight's standing threat against White's Queen Bishop Pawn at White's Queen Bishop 4 square. In addition, this Knight serves a useful defensive function in generally preventing the dynamic thrust P–Q5 or taking the sting out of it.

Black's *Queen Knight* has an ideal post at his Queen Bishop 3 square, where it exerts direct pressure on White's Queen Pawn. Sometimes Black plays . . . N–QN5 in order to gain time for . . . P–QB4 to break up White's Pawn center. Whether or not this stratagem proves successful will depend on the individual situation.

Black's *King Bishop* plays to King 2. When Black plays . . . P–KB3 and White replies KPxKBP, Black may recapture with his King Bishop in order to step up the pressure on White's Queen Pawn.

Black's *Queen Bishop* plays to King Bishop 4 early in the opening. (This is quite different from most situations in the

French Defense, where Black's Queen Bishop may be hemmed in for a long time.) Later on, Black's Queen Bishop may play to King Knight 5 to intensify the attack on White's Queen Pawn by threatening to remove White's King Knight.

Black's *Queen Rook* is logically best placed at Queen 1. In the case of Queen-side castling the Rook occupies the desired spot automatically. After King-side castling Black will play . . . QR–Q1.

Black's *King Rook* will come to King Bishop 1 in King-side castling.

Black's *Queen* often plays to Queen 2 to make room for a Black Rook at Queen 1 to intensify the pressure against White's Queen Pawn.

Black's *King* goes to King Knight 1 in King-side castling, where he is reasonably safe from attack. The King plays to Queen Bishop 1 in Queen-side castling, where he is generally exposed to a strong attack.

ILLUSTRATIVE GAMES

GAME 1

(gives us a good idea of White's resources against determined pressure on his center Pawns)

Match, 1939

WHITE	BLACK
W. Adams	*H. Morton*
1 P–K4	N–KB3
2 P–K5	N–Q4
3 P–QB4	N–N3
4 P–Q4	P–Q3
5 P–B4	PxP

          6   BPxP   N–B3
Black begins the work of demolishing White's Pawn center.
Naturally White must fight back energetically.

          7   B–K3   B–B4
          8   N–QB3   P–K3
          9   N–B3   . . .

Position after 9 N–B3
How does Black proceed?

Diagram 7

BLACK

WHITE

Now Black must make a definite choice. He can continue 9
. . . Q–Q2 with the idea of castling Queen-side. Or he can play
9 . . . B–K2 followed by castling on the King-side. Instead, he
chooses a third alternative, which involves an immediate attack
on White's Pawn center.

          9   . . .   N–N5
The threat of . . . N–B7ch gains time for Black.

         10   R–B1   P–B4
For White to reply 11 PxP would be poor play, in view of

the continuation 11 . . . QxQch; 12 KxQ, Castles ch followed
by 13 . . . N–Q2 when Black would regain his Pawn advantageously.

11   P–QR3   . . .

White practically forces Black's reply, for if 11 . . . N–B3?;
12 P–Q5 and Black has a strategically lost game.

11   . . .   PxP!

The only logical move. Note that on the reply 12 B–N5 Black
is prepared to give up his Queen: 12 . . . PxN!; 13 BxQ, PxP;
14 BxN, PxR/Q; 15 QxQ, N–B7ch; 16 K moves, PxB and Black
has the initiative and material compensation for his Queen.

Position after 11 . . . PxP!
Black is ready to sacrifice his Queen

Diagram 8

BLACK

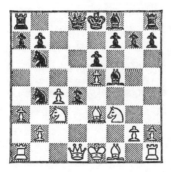

WHITE

12   NxP   . . .

Black has achieved his heart's desire in breaking up White's
Pawn center. But, as so often happens in this opening, White
has obtained an aggressive position.

12   . . .   N–B3

13   NxB!   . . .

Now Black can play 13 . . . QxQch; 14 RxQ, PxN; but after
15 N–N5 (threatening N–B7ch) he is in trouble. For example:
15 . . . R–B1; 16 NxP!, NxN; 17 BxN, N–B3; 18 P–B5!, NxP;
19 B–N5ch, N–B3; 20 Castles, P–N3; 21 KR–K1ch with a winning position for White.

13   . . .   PxN
14   Q–B3!   . . .

White does not trouble himself about loose Pawns, his object
being to press his advantage in mobility and set a trap or two
while he is at it.

For example, after 14 . . . P–N3 White gets a big positional
plus with 15 N–N5!, B–K2 (if 15 . . . NxKP; 16 QxNP is much
in White's favor); 16 N–Q6ch!, BxN; 17 PxB, etc. as Black
must not play 17 . . . QxP? because of 18 P–B5 winning a piece.

Black understandably finds these possibilities uninviting. He
therefore tries a tactical trick, only to find himself outsmarted by
White's subtle refutation.

14   . . .   NxBP?!
15   BxN   Q–R5ch
(*See Diagram 8*)

Black, it seems, expects 16 Q–B2 or 16 B–B2, in which case
16 . . . QxB is quite satisfactory as the reply 17 N–Q5 is ruled
out.

It is true that White can resort to 16 P–KN3, but then Black
escapes with 16 . . . QxB; 17 N–Q5, NxP!; 18 Q–N2, N–Q6ch;
19 K–Q2, NxR; 20 RxN, QxNch!; 21 QxQ, R–Q1. With two
Pawns ahead for the Exchange, Black should then win the resulting endgame.

16   K–Q2!!   . . .

This completely unexpected move changes the whole complexion of the game.

Position after 15 . . . Q–R5ch
Does Black's combination work?

Diagram 9

BLACK

WHITE

	16 . . .	QxB
	17 N–Q5!	. . .

The point. Black's Queen is attacked, while at the same time White threatens 18 N–B7ch winning Black's Queen Rook.

The reply 17 . . . Q–N6 is inadequate, for example 17 N–B7ch, K–Q2; 19 NxR, QxNPch; 20 R–B2, QxKP; 21 R–QN1 and wins.

	17 . . .	QxNch

Black has nothing better.

	18	QxQ	R–Q1
	19	QxRch	KxQ

White's material advantage assures him an easy win.

	20	KR–Q1	K–Q2
	21	K–K2 dis ch	K–K3
	22	R–Q3	B–K2

If Black plays 22 . . . NxP White has a convincing reply in 23 R–N3, P–QN3; 24 R–B7, etc.

23	R–N3	P–B5

Black sets two traps: if 24 BxBP?, N–Q5ch wins; or if 24 RxP?, N–Q1 wins.

24	B–B2	N–R4
25	R–N5	P–QN3
26	P–QN4	N–N2
27	R–B7	R–QN1
28	BxP!	. . .

For if 28 . . . PxB; 29 RxPch is crushing.

28	. . .	P–QR3
29	B–R7!	Resigns

After 29 . . . PxR; 30 BxR White's victory is only a matter of time.

GAME 2

(shows how Black can seize a powerful initiative by aggressive play)

Dortmund, 1929

WHITE	BLACK
R. *Spielmann*	E. *Colle*
1 P–K4	N–KB3
2 P–K5	N–Q4
3 P–QB4	N–N3
4 P–Q4	P–Q3
5 P–B4	PxP
6 BPxP	N–QB3
7 B–K3	B–B4
8 N–QB3	P–K3
9 B–K2	B–K2

Black has made his decision: he intends to castle King-side.

10	N–B3	Castles

11   Castles   P–B3

With this attack on White's imposing Pawn array in the center, Black anticipates some such continuation as 12 PxP, BxP; 13 Q–Q2, R–B2; 14 QR–Q1, R–Q2. In that case Black's pressure would be very promising, so White thinks of a different procedure.

Position after 11 . . . P–B3
Black anticipates an attack on White's center

Diagram 10

BLACK

WHITE

12   N–KR4!   . . .

White gives the game an unexpected turn.

12   . . .   PxP
13   NxB   PxN
14   P–Q5!   . . .

Apparently a difficult move to answer; for example 14 . . . N–R4; 15 BxN, RPxN; 16 P–QR3, P–B4; 17 N–N5. In this case Black's extra Pawn is meaningless and his Knight is in constant danger of going lost whenever White engineers P–QN4.

The alternative 14 . . . N–N1; 15 P–B5, N–B1; 16 Q–N3 is even worse for Black, thanks to the twofold threat of P–Q6 dis ch and QxP.

14 . . .   N–Q5!

Black wisely returns the Pawn.

15 BxN   PxB
16 QxP   N–Q2

Black gains time to get his Knight into active play by threatening to win White's Queen with . . . B–B4.

17 N–R4   . . .

White parries the threat and prepares to enforce P–B5. Much better, however, was 17 K–R1, leaving his Knight *with access to the center.*

17 . . .   P–QN4!

A masterly conception. Black splits White's Pawns, rules out White's P–B5, and prepares to centralize his forces. This is well worth a Pawn.

18 PxP   B–Q3
19 QR–K1   Q–K2!
20 B–Q3   . . .

The more modest 20 B–Q1 was better, giving White more secure protection against the coming inroads of Black's Knight.

(*See Diagram 11*)

20 . . .   N–K4!

The point of this clever move is that after 21 BxP, RxB!; 22 RxR, N–B6ch! followed by . . . QxRch Black has a winning attack.

21 K–R1   P–B5!

Naturally White must not reply 22 RxP?, RxR; 23 QxR, NxB and Black has won a piece.

22 R–K2   QR–K1!
23 N–B3   . . .

Position after 20 B–Q3
Must White win a Pawn?

Diagram 11

BLACK

WHITE

A pretty variation is 23 KR–K1, Q–R5; 24 RxN, QxRch! and Black wins.

White is at last bringing his banished Knight into the game, but it is too late.

    23 . . .   Q–R5
    24 N–K4   N–N5

Black's threat of . . . QxP mate is decisive. If White tries 25 P–KN3, Black has an easy win with 25 . . . Q–R6; 26 R–QB2, PxP, etc.

And on 25 Q–N1 Black wins neatly with 25 . . . NxP!; 26 QxN, QxQch; 27 KxQ, P–B6 dis ch, etc.

    25 P–KR3   . . .

The only alternative left to White. But Black's reply completes the demolition of White's position.

(See Diagram 12)

Position after 25 P–KR3
Black has a decisive break-through

Diagram 12

BLACK

WHITE

       25 . . .   **P–B6!**

A crushing stroke, for if White tries 26 PxP there follows 26 . . . QxPch; 27 K–N1, B–R7ch and Black mates in two more moves.

Nor does 26 R–QB2 help, in view of 26 . . . N–K4! threatening to win a piece with . . . NxB. If then 27 PxP (White has no good move), QxPch; 28 R–R2, QxR/R7ch!; 29 KxQ, NxP dbl ch followed by . . . NxQ and Black is a Rook to the good.

       26 RxP   **RxR**

White is in despair, for if 27 PxR, QxPch; 28 K–N1, B–R7ch and Black forces mate.

       27 N–B6ch   **K–B2!**
                     Resigns

For if 28 NxN, R–B8ch forces the game. Or 28 RxR, RxPch! and Black has a quick mate. Black's brilliant success was well deserved.

Some useful pointers

For White:

1. Be aggressive, but not at the cost of compromising the advanced center Pawns.

2. Be especially careful to guard your Queen Pawn adequately.

3. Develop your Queen Knight before the King Knight, and play B–K2 before N–KB3—all this to take the sting out of a possible Black . . . B–KN5.

4. Avoid P–QB5 which looks tempting but only forces Black to transfer his Knight from the poor post Queen Knight 3 to the fine square Queen 4.

For Black:

1. Concentrate on White's Queen Pawn as a target.

2. Aim for . . . P–QB4 or . . . P–KB3 as a means of breaking up White's Pawn center.

3. Make a point of striving to get your Knight away from Queen Knight 3 and onto a better square.

4. Look for tactical opportunities to exploit the advanced state of White's center Pawns.

Conclusions

In recent years the popularity of this defense has declined steeply. This implies a collective judgment on the part of the masters. It is apparently their view that the plus features of White's advanced center outweigh the negative features.

There are, however, some specialized reasons for adopting the defense. It is suitable for adoption against a weaker player who is sure to lack the resourcefulness this defense demands from White and Black as well.

The defense has surprise value. There is also a psychological

challenge involved—adoption of this tricky defense serves notice
that you mean to play a hard, complicated game with no quarter
given. If pursued along these lines, the defense offers good
prospects of success.

Lesson 6

QUEEN'S GAMBIT DECLINED

(Orthodox Defense)

WHITE	BLACK
1 P–Q4	P–Q4
2 P–QB4	P–K3

This line of play is one of the most solid and most dependable defenses to the Queen's Gambit Declined. Yet it results in certain basic problems for Black, as we can see from the following diagram picture of the Normal Pawn Skeleton.

The Normal Pawn Skeleton

Diagram 1

BLACK

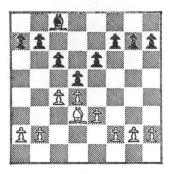

WHITE

The ordinary player may glean very little from this outline of the typical Pawn formation. The master, on the other hand, finds this scheme very informative. You can follow in the footsteps of the master by asking yourself, What are the Bishops doing in Diagram 1?

The answer is illuminating. White's Bishop, which moves on white squares, is eminently mobile. This Bishop is not hemmed in by the White Pawns on black squares.

But consider the situation of the Black Bishop. This Bishop cannot develop properly, *because it is hemmed in by several Black Pawns placed on white squares.*

So here we have a perfect example of the all-important role of the Pawn skeleton determining the course of the game. If Black is to get a satisfactory position, he must remove one of the obstacles to the development of his Bishop. Basically, there are two possible techniques for creating freedom of action for the Black Bishop. One of them is shown in Diagram 1a.

Black has created an open diagonal for his Bishop

Diagram 1a

BLACK

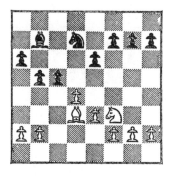

WHITE

Just what did Black have to do to develop his Bishop in this beautifully effective manner?

This is what he did:

(a) His Queen Pawn captured White's Queen Bishop Pawn and White retook with his Bishop.

(b) Black then played . . . P–QR3.

(c) When it was his turn to play again, he continued . . . P–QN4, gaining time by driving away White's Bishop.

(d) The next step in Black's liberating maneuver was to play . . . P–QB4. At this point he had created a fine, free diagonal for his "problem" Bishop.

(e) Finally with all his preparations completed, Black played . . . B–N2, giving his Bishop a clear diagonal and enabling it to bear down powerfully against the center.

Now for the alternative way of freeing Black's Bishop:

Again Black has freed his Bishop

Diagram 1b

BLACK

WHITE

In this case Black's procedure was much simpler. He played

. . . QPxQBP as before, and then continued . . . P–K4, creating
a diagonal for his problem Bishop.

The above is a greatly simplified explanation of what Black
must do to free his Bishop. In the foregoing explanation most
of the pieces have been removed from the board, in order to
focus the reader's attention on the basic aspects of the problem.

In actual play it is much more difficult to solve the problem—
in fact, it is much more difficult to know what the problem is!
—with a great many pieces on the board. Let's therefore see how
the crucial position comes into being, and how it leads to the
problem of freeing the Bishop.

Basic variations

WHITE	BLACK
1 P–Q4	P–Q4
2 P–QB4	. . .

Position after 2 P–QB4
The Typical Queen's Gambit Move

Diagram 2

BLACK

WHITE

This is the typical offer of the Queen's Gambit. White offers a Pawn, for after 2 . . . PxP Black's Pawn would be gone from the center, leaving White with a Pawn monopoly of the center.

Let's dwell on this problem for a moment: suppose Black accepts the gambit with 2 . . . PxP. How does White proceed? Well, if he is bothered about "losing" a Pawn he can simply continue 3 Q–R4ch, picking up Black's foremost Queen Bishop Pawn at his leisure.

But White has other possibilities, for example 3 P–K4—which, however, looks stronger than it really is. For then comes 3 . . . P–K4!; 4 PxP, QxQch; 5 KxQ, B–K3 and Black is not too badly off.

Should White proceed more conservatively? Suppose he tries 3 P–K3. But then Black can play 3 . . . P–K4! and free himself. However, note the amusing trap 4 BxP, PxP; 5 N–KB3, PxP???; 6 BxPch! and White wins the Queen! But Black plays 5 . . . P–QB4 or 5 . . . P–K3 with a fair game.

White's best course after 2 . . . PxP is simple development with 3 N–KB3, which, by the way, stops . . . P–K4.

Let's recapitulate. We have 1 P–Q4, P–Q4; 2 P–QB4, PxP; 3 N–KB3. Now suppose Black wants to hold on to his "won" Pawn with 3 . . . P–QN4. We smash up his Pawn position with 4 P–QR4, P–QB3 (if 4 . . . P–QR3; 5 PxP and Black must not retake—why?); 5 P–QN3! and Black's Queen-side Pawns are in a bad way.

An interesting possibility is 5 . . . B–R3 (stubborn!); 6 RPxP, P(B3)xP; 7 PxP, PxP; 8 RxB!, NxR; 9 Q–R4ch, Q–Q2; 10 QxN. Having gained two pieces for a Rook, White is the one who is ahead in material.

The moral of these hypothetical moves is that in offering the gambit, White need observe only reasonable care to be sure of recovering his material advantageously.

Now back to Diagram 2.

2 . . .   P–K3

Black wants to be sure of having a Pawn in the center: if White continues 3 PxP, Black replies 3 . . . PxP.

So far, so good. But now Black has set up his typical problem in this variation: *he has blocked the development of his Queen Bishop.*

Position after 2 . . . P–K3
How is Black to develop his Queen Bishop?

Diagram 3

BLACK

WHITE

The order in which the following moves are played may vary considerably, but it all boils down to the Basic Position shown in Diagram 5.

3 N–QB3   N–KB3

Both these Knight moves are part of the struggle for control of that vital center square White's King 4 (Black's King 5).

4 B–N5   . . .

By pinning Black's Knight, White puts that piece out of action—from the point of view of the pinned Knight's inability to exert pressure on the center.

Black can rid himself of the pin by playing 4 . . . B–K2, but he prefers instead to set a fascinating trap.

4 . . .   QN–Q2

This is the trappy move. It seems senseless, as White can reply 5 PxP, PxP; 6 NxP winning a Pawn.

Position after 4 . . . QN–Q2
Can White win a Pawn?

Diagram 4

BLACK

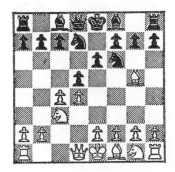

WHITE

The attempt by White to win a Pawn would end in catastrophe for him: 5 PxP, PxP; 6 NxP?? (White relies on the pin), NxN!! (the proverbial bolt from the blue); 7 BxQ (has Black blundered?), B–N5ch! (no, for now Black wins White's Queen and comes out a piece ahead).

So White must proceed more discreetly.

5 P–K3   . . .

Now White really threatens to win the Pawn, as Black's Queen sacrifice would no longer work. So Black provides additional protection for his Queen Pawn.

5	. . .	B–K2
6	N–B3	Castles
7	R–B1	. . .

A characteristic move in this variation. White prepares to exert pressure along the Queen Bishop file. At present this pressure is intangible and potential, but it has made itself felt in many a game.

7	. . .	P–B3

Black neutralizes the possible pressure along the Queen Bishop file—at least for the time being—and at the same time prepares to develop his Queen Bishop.

Position after 7 . . . P–B3
The Basic Position

Diagram 5

BLACK

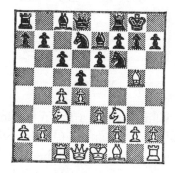

WHITE

As we saw in the discussions of Diagrams 1a and 1b, Black will try to free his Queen Bishop for action either by preparing for . . . P–K4 or by preparing for the fianchetto of the Bishop. The resulting possibilities will become clearer to us from the discussion of the Normal Formation and the Illustrative Games.

White's Normal Formation

White's *King Rook Pawn* remains at King Rook 2.

White's *King Knight Pawn* likewise remains at King Knight 2.

White's *King Bishop Pawn* generally remains on its original square, but there are some characteristic situations in which the Pawn advances to King Bishop 4. This advance may serve any or all of the following purposes:

(1) to support a White Knight at King 5. As a rule, this central square is a very strong post for a Knight. It forms a useful element in a formidable King-side attack. Another valuable aspect of supporting the advanced Knight with P–KB4 is that if Black plays . . . NxN, White can reply KBPxN on King 5, opening up the King Bishop file for his Rooks—generally with devastating effect.

(2) P–KB4 is sometimes played to restrain Black from freeing himself with . . . P–K4.

(3) When P–KB4 is played as a follow-up to N–K5, it has the additional virtue of making room for the maneuver R–KB3–KR3. In conjunction with the action of White's Bishop at Queen 3, this has been known to result in many a vicious attack which left White without adequate defense.

White's *King Pawn* plays to King 3 in order to make room for the development of White's King Bishop to Queen 3. (Caution: defer P–K3 until you have played out your Queen Bishop to King Knight 5.) In some cases the King Pawn, when properly supported, may advance to King 4 in the middle-game stage.

White's *Queen Pawn* plays to the commanding center square Queen 4, generally on White's first move. Here the Pawn controls the important King 5 and Queen Bishop 5 squares. This serves the valuable strategic objectives of preventing . . . P–K4 and . . . P–QB4.

Through a series of Pawn exchanges, White's Queen Pawn

can sometimes become isolated. In that case, the Pawn serves as a strong support for a White Knight on King 5 and also as a target for Black's pieces.

White's *Queen Bishop Pawn* plays to Queen Bishop 4 very early in the game to entice Black's Queen Pawn away from the center—as we have already seen. Consequently, Black's . . . QPxQBP is only permissible when Black plays it as part of a far-reaching plan to free his game and develop his Queen Bishop. The Illustrative Games are illuminating on these points.

White's *Queen Knight Pawn* generally remains at its home square. There are times, however, when it may advance to Queen Knight 4 to prevent Black from freeing himself with . . . P–QB4.

White's *Queen Rook Pawn* does not advance as a rule. There are two kinds of typical situations, though, in which it may conceivably advance. One is to play P–QR4 to try to bring confusion into Black's ranks when a Black Pawn is placed at Black's Queen Knight 4 square. Also, when White has played P–QN4 he may precede or follow up this advance with P–QR3, guarding his Queen Knight Pawn.

As for White's pieces:

White's *King Knight* takes up an effective post by developing to King Bishop 3. Here it guards White's valuable Queen Pawn and brings pressure to bear on the important square King 5. As already indicated, the maneuver N–K5 often places White's Knight on a powerfully centralized post.

White's *Queen Knight* is strongly placed at Queen Bishop 3. Later on in the middle game it often happens that this Knight can be strongly centralized at King 4. From here it may move on to King Knight 5 for attacking purposes, or it may remain on King 4 to restrain the freeing move . . . P–QB4.

In other cases, after Black has played . . . QPxQBP, White's

Knight on Queen Bishop 3 supports the advance of White's King Pawn to King 4.

White's *Queen Bishop*, as we have seen, plays to King Knight 5 quite early in the opening. In general the Bishop exerts a very cramping effect on Black's position. Compare its effective, early development with the difficulties confronting its Black colleague. Note also the cautionary comment in our treatment of the King Pawn: you must avoid thoughtlessly playing P–K3 *before* developing your Queen Bishop; for in that case you will find that you have blocked the development of the Bishop. This is illustrated in Diagram 6.

Each Queen Bishop is hemmed in by the respective King Pawn

Diagram 6

BLACK

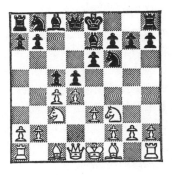

WHITE

White's *King Bishop* plays to Queen 3, a pivotal post at which the Bishop plays an important role in the center; while at the same time it is ready for King-side attack along the diagonal Queen 3–King Rook 7 as well as for Queen-side positional play along the diagonal Queen 3–Queen Rook 6. (The latter possibility is effectively underscored in the second Illustrative Game.)

Thanks mainly to Black's capture . . . QPxQBP, White's King Bishop often reaches the Queen Bishop 4 square. Here, in combination with a well-centralized Knight at Queen Bishop 4, the Bishop may take part in the creating of threats on the diagonal Queen Rook 2–King Knight 8.

White's King Bishop has still another possible means of development. In games of a predominantly positional, maneuvering character, the Bishop often plays to King Bishop 3 via King 2. This is what happens in the first Illustrative Game.

White's *Rooks* present something of a problem to the inexperienced player, as there are several ways to deploy them. Let's consider the alternative possibilities:

(1) If Black plays . . . QPxQBP, White gets a half-open Queen Bishop file and the potential advance P–Q5 becomes at least something to think about. In that event White's Rooks seem most strongly placed at Queen Bishop 1 and Queen 1 (Diagram 6a).

(2) If Black plays . . . QPxQBP and White, having Pawn control of the center, advances P–K4–K5, we get a different kind of position. Once at King 5, the Pawn makes it impossible for Black to defend his beleaguered King-side with . . . N–KB3. White then has strong attacking possibilities. So he might leave his King Rook at King Bishop 1 and continue with QR–K1. This might involve such subsequent maneuvers as R–K4–KN4, or P–KB4 followed by R–KB3–KR3–in either case with a crushing attack. See Diagram 6b.

In this setup some players prefer to continue more conservatively: KR–K1 (to take part in the King-side attack) and QR–Q1 (to guard the backward White Queen Pawn. Even this may take an aggressive form via R–Q1–Q3–KN3 and again White is aiming for King-side attack).

White has advanced P–Q5 effectively

Diagram 6a

BLACK

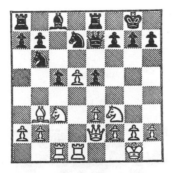

WHITE

White plays for a King-side attack

Diagram 6b

BLACK

WHITE

(3) White may get an isolated Pawn in this manner: Black plays . . . QPxPxQBP; then he continues . . . P–QB4 followed

by . . . QBPxQP, to which White replies KPxQP. The likely placement of White's Rooks in that event would be at King 1 (for aggressive purposes) and QR–Q1 (to support the isolated Queen Pawn).

Typical formation with an isolated Pawn

Diagram 6c

BLACK

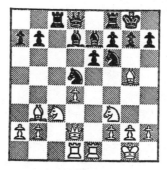

WHITE

White's *Queen* has a mobility which contributes vitally to the strength of this opening. Her best square is King 2. It serves as a pivot point for action on both wings.

White's *King* goes to King Knight 1 in the course of castling.

Black's Normal Formation

Black's *King Rook Pawn* generally remains on its home square. On occasion Black plays . . . P–KR3; but later on he may find that he has seriously weakened his castled position.

Black's *King Knight Pawn* should remain at King Knight 2 to avoid a weakening of his castled position.

Black's *King Bishop Pawn* should likewise remain unmoved.
This is particularly important in the case of the King Bishop
Pawn, as the frequently encountered . . . P–KB4 weakens Black's
Pawn position sadly by creating a "hole" at his King 4 square.
That is to say, with both Black's Queen Pawn and King Bishop
Pawn advanced to the fourth rank, Black has no Pawn left with
which to prevent access of White pieces to his King 4 square.
The consequence is shown in Diagram 7.

Black's King 4 square is a "hole"

Diagram 7

BLACK

WHITE

Black's *King Pawn* plays to King 3 very early in the opening.
Later on, Black may attempt to enforce . . . P–K4 in order to be
able to develop his Queen Bishop.

Black's *Queen Pawn* always goes to Queen 4—generally on
the very first move. Later on, Black generally plays . . .
QPxQBP. It is a good idea to defer this exchange until White
has played B–Q3; in that way Black gains a move, as it then
takes White's Bishop two moves to reach Queen Bishop 4.

Black's *Queen Bishop Pawn* goes to Queen Bishop 3 in the opening, for a variety of reasons. After White's R–B1, Black's . . . P–QB3 serves to neutralize White's pressure along the Queen Bishop file—at least for the time being.

A little later, once Black has played . . . QPxQBP and White has replied BxP, Black's Pawn at Queen Bishop 3 supports the freeing maneuvers . . . P–QN4 (Game 1) or . . . N–Q4 (Game 2).

In any event, Black's long-term goal as regards his Queen Bishop Pawn must be to play . . . P–QB4 in the early middle game. This gives his Rooks a chance to exert a fair amount of influence along the Queen Bishop file, which has already been opened halfway on White's side of the board, and can now be opened from Black's side as well.

The other function of . . . P–QB4 is to open the diagonal of Black's fianchettoed Queen Bishop (see Diagram 1a).

Black's *Queen Knight Pawn* may go QN4 (Game 1) or to QN3 (Game 2) in order to make room for the development of his Queen Bishop at Queen Knight 2.

Black's *Queen Rook Pawn* is moved or ignored depending on what happens to his Queen Knight Pawn. Thus . . . P–QN3 does not call for any accompanying move from Black's Queen Rook Pawn. On the other hand, . . . P–QN4 is almost invariably preceded by . . . P–QR3.

As for Black's pieces:

Black's *King Knight* goes to King Bishop 3 where it takes part in the fight for control of important center squares: Black's King 5 and Queen 4 squares.

To develop this Knight to King 2, by the way, would be very bad: the Knight would not control King 5 and it would impede the development of Black's King Bishop to King 2.

Black's *Queen Knight* goes to Queen 2. (The ordinarily more desirable square Queen Bishop 3 is, as we have seen, reserved for

Black's Queen Bishop Pawn.) The Queen Knight plays a vitally important role in supporting the strategically vital advance . . . P–K4 or . . . P–QB4.

Black's *King Bishop* is developed at King 2. This is generally the case when a positional or defensive game is contemplated.

Black's *Queen Bishop,* as we have seen from the discussions of Diagrams 1a and 1b, is the "problem child" of his development scheme. The Illustrative Games show how the Bishop is developed on Queen Knight 2. A note in Game 2 shows how the Bishop can be developed along its natural diagonal after . . . P–K4.

Black's *Rooks* are generally developed to Queen 1 and Queen Bishop 1. Then, if file-opening occurs, the Black Rooks are prepared to do their part on the newly opened lines.

Black's *Queen* generally goes to King 2 by recapturing after White's Queen Bishop is exchanged for Black's King Bishop as a result of . . . N–Q4. (This is shown in the Illustrative Games.)

Black's *King* goes to King Knight 1 in the course of castling.

ILLUSTRATIVE GAMES

GAME 1

(shows how White gains the advantage because of his much greater mobility)

New York, 1934

WHITE	BLACK
F. Reinfeld	C. Byrne
1 P–QB4	N–KB3

What, the reader may ask, do these moves have to do with the variation we are studying?

Obviously the game has not started as a Queen's Pawn opening. The fact is that these rather mysterious moves are "feelers." For the moment, neither player is revealing his intentions; yet the moves are such that the opening may yet "transpose" into a Queen's Gambit Declined of orthodox format.

Formally, White's first move is known as the English Opening. Had Black replied with 1 . . . P–K4, we would definitively have an English Opening. Instead, he has selected a noncommittal reply which still leaves the eventual opening up in the air.

Position after 1 . . . N–KB3
What will the opening be?

Diagram 8

BLACK

WHITE

    2 N–QB3   P–B3
    3 P–Q4   P–Q4

Now we know that the opening is a Queen's Gambit Declined. But Black has yet to play . . . P–K3, the move characteristic of the Orthodox Defense.

    4 N–B3   . . .

This line of play (. . . P–QB3 without . . . P–K3) is known as the Slav Defense.

4 . . .   P–K3

Only after this move are we in the realm of the Orthodox Defense.

5   B–N5   QN–Q2
6   P–K3   B–K2
7   R–B1   Castles

And now we have the Basic Position (Diagram 5) of the Orthodox Defense.

8   B–Q3   PxP

Now that White has moved his King Bishop, Black makes the capture, gaining a move.

9   BxBP   P–N4
10 B–Q3   P–QR3

Position after 10 . . . P–QR3
Black is preparing to develop his Queen Bishop

Diagram 9

BLACK

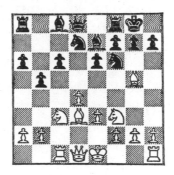

WHITE

Instead of waiting serenely while Black carries out his intentions, White decides to intervene boldly.

11   P–QR4!   . . .

Played with the idea of crossing Black's intentions. However, if Black reacts with 11 . . . P–N5 (the natural reply), White can go wrong with 12 N–K4 (looks strong), NxN; 13 BxB, NxP! (now if 14 BxQ, NxQ or 14 KxN, QxB and in either case Black is a Pawn ahead); 14 BxPch (at least this maintains material equality), K–R1! (but not 14 . . . KxB???; 15 Q–B2ch! and Black loses his Queen); 15 KxN, QxB and Black has a playable game.

The right way after 11 . . . P–N5 is 12 BxN!, NxB; 13 N–K4 and no matter how Black plays, he can never advance his backward Queen Bishop Pawn. He would therefore have a positionally lost game.

11   . . .   B–Nt2

At last this Bishop is developed, but in rather an indifferent manner, as it is blocked by Black's Queen Bishop Pawn. Everything stands or falls now by the advance of this Pawn.

12   Castles   R–B1
13   Q–K2!   . . .

Obviously Black cannot play 13 . . . P–B4, as White simply replies 14 RPxP, winning a Pawn.

So perhaps Black should play 13 . . . P–N5 first, but after the reply 14 N–K4 he is still in trouble. For if then 14 . . . NxN; 15 BxB, QxB; 16 BxN, N–B3; 17 B–Q3, P–QR4; 18 B–R6! Black is in very serious trouble, as he cannot advance his weak Queen Bishop Pawn and meanwhile White threatens to strengthen the pressure along the Queen Bishop file by simply continuing R–B2 followed by KR–B1.

At first sight it seems as if Black might be better off with 13 . . . P–N5; 14 N–K4, Q–R4; for in this way Black guards his own Queen Rook Pawn, counterattacks against White's Queen Rook Pawn, and supports the possibility . . . P–B4. Yet even the

Position after 13 Q–K2!
Can Black advance his backward Queen Bishop Pawn?

Diagram 10

BLACK

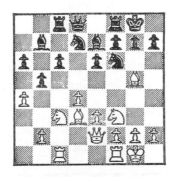

WHITE

combination of these factors does not quite turn the trick for
Black after 15 NxNch. For example:

I 15 . . . PxN; 16 B–R6, KR–Q1; 17 P–QN3, P–QB4
(success, so it seems); 18 N–Q2! (threatening to win at once
with Q–N4ch, etc.), P–B4; 19 N–B4, Q–B2; 20 B–B4, Q–B3
(threatens mate); 21 P–B3 with a very strong game for White,
who has a winning reply to 21 . . . PxP in 22 N–Q6!, etc.

II 15 . . . NxN; 16 N–K5!, P–B4 (not 16 . . . QxP??; 17
R–R1, Q–N6; 18 B–QB4 winning Black's Queen); 17 BxN,
PxB (if 17 . . . BxB; 18 N–Q7 winning at least a Pawn); 18
Q–N4ch, K–R1; 19 Q–R4 and White wins.

Or try 15 . . . NxN; 16 N–K5!, KR–Q1; 17 BxN, BxB; 18
BxPch!, KxB; 19 Q–R5ch, K–N1; 20 QxPch and White wins.

III 15 . . . BxN; 16 BxB, NxB; 17 P–QN3, N–Q2 (if 17
. . . P–B4; 18 PxP, RxP; 19 RxR, QxR; 20 BxP and White has
won a Pawn); 18 N–K5!, NxN; 19 R–B5!, Q–N3; 20 RxN
and White has crushing pressure against Black's backward Queen
Bishop Pawn. Black would still lose a Pawn with 20 . . . P–

QB4, which means that White has time to strengthen the pressure with 21 R–QB5 followed by 22 KR–QB1 with a positionally won game.

To sum up: the hope of enforcing . . . P–B4 by preceding it with 13 . . . P–N5 proves impossible to carry out successfully. Black therefore tries a different freeing method.

13 . . .   N–Q4

Position after 13 . . . N–Q4
White is hard put to it to maintain a positional advantage

Diagram 11

BLACK

WHITE

At first sight it seems that White ought to continue 14 BxB, QxB; 15 NxN, KPxN (forced) and Black is left with a very weak Queen-side Pawn formation—not to mention the fact that his Bishop is buried alive.

But after 14 BxB Black interpolates 14 . . . NxN! and does not come off too badly. So White chooses a different method.

14 N–K4   . . .

Note that White is threatening to secure a marked positional advantage with 15 N–Q6!

15	. . .	P–R3
16	BxB	QᴀB

Black means to free his game now with . . . P–K4. White is
equally determined to nip this plan in the bud.

16	N–B5	NxN
17	RxN	. . .

Position after 17 RxN
White has won the first round

Diagram 12

BLACK

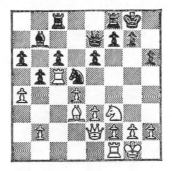

WHITE

White seems to have won the positional struggle, . . . P–K4
or . . . P–QB4 being impossible. It is true that 17 . . . PxP
would now be quite bad because of 18 BxP, but, nevertheless,
Black finds a most ingenious resource.

17	. . .	N–N3

Black's threat of . . . NxP clears the situation nicely for him.

18	PxP	. . .

Played with very great reluctance on White's part, for now
Black's Bishop finally comes to life.

18   . . .   BPxP

Black has acquired a beautiful diagonal for his Bishop, but if
he thinks his troubles are over, he is sadly mistaken; the conflict
is merely transferred to a different plane.

For, as we shall soon discover, White has three noticeable
positional advantages: he will have a strong game on the open
Queen Bishop file; he can develop powerful pressure on the black
squares; and his formidable Pawn center may result eventually
in a passed Queen Pawn (after P–K4).

Nor need White fear Black's Queen-side majority of Pawns
here; these Pawns cannot be effectively mobilized.

Position after 18 . . . BPxP
Black is by no means out of trouble

Diagram 13

BLACK

WHITE

19   KR–B1   N–R5

Black naturally wants to drive off the foremost White Rook
from its commanding post.

20   RxR   RxR
21   RxRch   BxR

22   Q–B2!   . . .

White takes the open file.

22   . . .   B–N2

23   N–K5!   . . .

White intensifies his hold on the black squares. This Knight cannot be dislodged by 23 . . . P–B3?? for then White wins Black's Queen with 24 B–R7ch and 25 N–N6ch.

23   . . .   N–N3

24   B–K2!   N–Q4

25   B–R5!   . . .

Forcing a further weakness on the black squares in Black's camp, as 25 . . . P–B3?? is refuted by 26 B–B7ch and 27 N–N6ch.

25   . . .   P–N3

26   B–B3   . . .

After 26 BxP, PxB; 27 QxPch, K–B1; 28 QxRPch White has three Pawns for the piece but no clear win.

26   . . .   N–N5

27   Q–Q1   BxB

28   QxB   N–Q4

To prevent a possible invasion by Q–R8ch, etc.

(See Diagram 14.)

Even at this late stage, with so much simplification having taken place, it would be a mistake to think that Black is finally safe.

29   P–K4!   . . .

Such is the strength of a powerful Pawn center that its formidable nature asserts itself even at this late date. Consequence: White gains ground.

29   . . .   N–N3

30   Q–B3!   . . .

White seizes the open file and threatens to obtain a clearly

Now White steadily gains ground

Diagram 14

BLACK

WHITE

winning position with 31 Q–B6, Q–R2; 32 P–Q5. In that case White's resulting passed Pawn would simply march in.

30   ...   Q–N2

31   P–B3   ...

White protects his King Pawn and also prepares to bring his King to the center.

31   ...   Q–B1

Black is understandably uncomfortable and therefore tries to neutralize White's control of the Queen Bishop file.

32   N–B6!   ...

White threatens to win the Queen with the nasty forking check N–K7ch, etc.

32   ...   Q–B2

33   Q–B5!   ...

More infiltration! And meanwhile White again threatens to win the Queen with N–K7ch. This combination of tactical and strategical methods is a characteristic means of exploiting superior mobility.

33 . . .   K–N2

Position after 33 . . . K–N2
White must exploit his own Pawns and neutralize Black's

Diagram 15

BLACK

WHITE

34 N–N4!   . . .

Black has been hoping for an exchange of Queens, and he can now have it—at the cost of a Pawn: 34 . . . QxQ?; 35 PxQ, and White wins the Queen Rook Pawn with easy victory in sight.

34 . . .   Q–N2
35 N–Q3!   N–Q2
36 Q–Q6!   . . .

Stronger than the plausible 36 Q–K7, which could have been answered with 36 . . . Q–B3.

Incidentally, White now threatens 37 N–B5, NxN; 38 PxN and the passed Pawn marches right in.

36 . . .   N–N3
37 P–QN3!   . . .

Immobilizing Black's Knight.

Position after 37 P–QN3!
At last Black blunders

Diagram 16

BLACK

WHITE

37 . . .   P–QR4

Black finally collapses under the strain of conducting a long
and arduous defense. However, after 37 . . . 38 K–N1; 38
N–B5, Q–R2; 39 K–B1! (not 39 P–Q5, PxP; 40 PxP, N–Q2!)
followed by P–Q5 White would win without too much trouble.

38 Q–K5ch   K–R2
39 QxNP   Q–R2
40 N–B5   . . .

White prevents . . . P–R5.

40 . . .   K–N2
41 K–B2   P–K4!?

Black hopes for 42 PxP, N–Q2; 43 QxN, QxNch when
Black can draw.

42 K–K3!   PxPch
43 KxP   . . .

The ironic consequence of Black's thrust for freedom is that
White's King is magnificently centralized.

43 KxP   P–R4

After this Black's game gallops rapidly downhill. The best chance was 43 . . . Q–B2 when White would still have to play with great care.

44 Q–B6!   . . .

With this important move White prevents . . . Q–B2.

44 . . .   P–QR5

This looks senseless, but Black realizes that 44 . . . Q–N1; 45 P–K5, Q–Q1ch; 46 Q–Q6, QxQch; 47 PxQ, K–B3; 48 N–R4, N–Q2; 49 K–Q5 is drearily hopeless for him.

45 PxP   Q–R4
46 K–Q3!   Q–N5

Black's faint hopes of a perpetual check are soon dispelled.

47 Q–N5!   Q–R6ch
48 K–B2   Resigns

For Black realizes that 48 . . . Q–R7ch would be answered by 47 Q–N2ch forcing the exchange of Queens. And in any event, with two Pawns down, Black finds himself in a hopeless situation.

GAME 2

(shows how Black finds himself in difficulties because he does not free his Queen Bishop promptly)

Hastings, 1922

WHITE	BLACK
E. Bogolyubov	*F. D. Yates*

1 P–Q4   P–Q4
2 P–QB4   P–K3

This time the game starts in a straightforward manner, without the subtle transpositions we saw in the first game.

3 N–KB3   N–KB3

4 N–B3   B–K2
5 B–N5   Castles
6 P–K3   QN–Q2

An alternative idea here, worthy of the student's attention, is the freeing maneuver 6 . . . N–K5; 7 BxB, QxB; 8 PxP, NxN; 9 PxN, PxP when Black has freed himself nicely and opened the diagonal of his Queen Bishop.

Position after 6 . . . QN–Q2
Both players are heading for the Basic Position

Diagram 17

BLACK

WHITE

7 R–B1   P–B3

And so we have arrived at the situation of Diagram 5.

8 Q–B2   . . .

An interesting finesse. White avoids the immediate B–Q3, for then there follows 8 . . . PxP; 9 BxBP and White has lost a move by moving his Bishop twice.

Now Black in turn might continue "the struggle for the tempo" by marking time, say with 8 . . . R–K1. Instead he plays . . . PxP, allowing White to gain a move by getting his Bishop to Queen Bishop 4 all in one move.

8 . . .   PxP

From what has just been said, we can see that this is an inaccuracy—not a fatal one, but it does make Black's task more difficult.

9   BxP   N–Q4

Black's characteristic freeing maneuver. No matter how White replies, Black gets greater maneuvering space.

10   BxB   QxB

11   Castles   NxN

12   QxN   . . .

Position after 12 *QxN*

The freeing move . . . P–K4 is not available

Diagram 18

BLACK

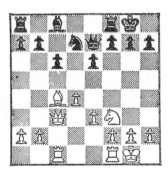

WHITE

In this position, you observe, Black cannot play 12 . . . P–K4? as it would simply lose a Pawn.

But suppose he had played 8 . . . R–K1. In that case the game might have continued 9 B–Q3, PxP; 10 BxBP, N–Q4; 11 BxB, QxB; 12 Castles, NxN; 13 QxN and now, because Black's Rook is at King 1, he can free himself with . . . P–K4.

The above, unfortunately, is only what Black should have done—not what he actually did. So let's return to the actual situation in Diagram 18.

If Black cannot free his Queen Bishop by . . . P–K4, he must find another way. The only alternative method is by fianchettoing the Bishop. Hence Black's next two moves.

12 . . .   P–QN3
13 Q–Q3   . . .

White's idea is to answer 13 . . . B–N2 with 14 B–R6, forcing an exchange of Bishops after which the white squares in Black's Queen-side might turn out to be weak. Nevertheless 13 . . . P–QB4 is quite playable and would put Black well on the way to equality.

13 . . .   R–Q1

With this sly move Black only overreaches himself. The idea is that 14 B–R6?? is refuted by 14 . . . N–B4. But the only result is that White shifts his Queen to a safer square, so Black's Rook move is really a waste of time.

14 Q–K2   . . .

Now again Black should strive for equality with . . . P–QB4, but again he loses valuable time, and—worse yet—creates a weakness.

(See Diagram 19)

14 . . .   P–QR3

This prevents B–R6, but it weakens Black's Queen Knight Pawn and gives White time to accumulate pressure against Black's Queen-side.

15 B–Q3!   . . .

Position after 14 Q–K2
Black should free his game with . . . P–QB4

Diagram 19

BLACK

WHITE

Now Black's position has become difficult. His Queen Bishop Pawn is attacked, and if he plays 15 . . . P–QB4 there follows 16 B–K4, R–R2; 17 B–B6 (threatens BxN followed by PxP, leaving Black with fatally weak Pawns), PxP; 18 PxP and Black's troubles are far from over. He cannot, for example, play 18 . . . B–N2, as this would lose a Pawn.

15	. . .	B–N2
16	B–K4	QR–B1
17	R–B3!	. . .

White builds up the pressure relentlessly. Now he threatens 18 Q–B2, winning a Pawn directly.

| 17 | . . . | N–B3 |

Black could ward off the threat with 17 . . . P–KB4 also, but in that event he would be enhancing his Pawn weaknesses.

18	B–Q3	N–Q4
19	QR–B1	N–N5
20	B–B4	. . .

It has seemed during the last few moves that Black was gaining time all along the line, but the fact remains that White is still threatening to win a Pawn (with 21 P–QR3).

20 . . .   P–QR4

Now Black threatens to win a Pawn with 21 . . . P–QN4; 22 B–N3, P–R5. But White parries the threat with the greatest ease and then goes on to carry out his own strategical plans.

21   P–QR3   N–Q4

22   B–R6!   . . .

White obtains an overwhelming strategical advantage

Diagram 20

BLACK

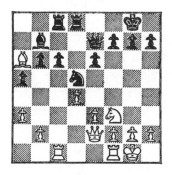

WHITE

By forcing the exchange of Bishops, White uncovers the critical weakness of Black's Queen Bishop Pawn. Black's Queen Knight Pawn is not much better off.

22 . . .   BxB

Black's game is strategically lost. The only remaining question is, how and where the final blow will fall.

23   QxB   R–R1

White was threatening to win a Pawn with 24 P–K4.

24 Q–R4   QR–B1

To play the other Rook here is slightly better, but Black's reluctance to take up a completely defensive position is quite understandable.

25 N–K5   . . .

By threatening NxQBP, White forces the following advance with a further deterioration of Black's Pawn position.

25 . . .   P–QB4

26 Q–R6   . . .

Now White threatens to win easily with 27 P–K4, N–B3; 28 QxNP, NxP; 29 KR–K1, R–N1; 30 N–B6!, etc.

26 . . .   Q–Q3

Black provides additional support for his menaced Queen Knight Pawn.

27 KR–Q1   . . .

The immediate N–B4 is also good enough to win.

27 . . .   R–R1

Likewise after 27 . . . R–N1; 28 N–B4, Q–B2; 29 PxP, QxBP; 30 N–K5 Black has no good move.

28 Q–N7   . . .

(See Diagram 21)

White threatens 29 N–B6 followed by 30 P–K4, N–B5; 31 PxP and wins. Or 29 N–B6 followed by 30 PxP, PxP; 31 P–K4 and wins.

28 . . .   N–K2?

29 N–B4   Resigns

For after 29 . . . Q–Q2; 30 QxQ, RxQ; 31 NxNP Black's los of material leaves him with a hopeless game.

Position after 28 Q–N7
Black is left without a satisfactory move

Diagram 21

BLACK

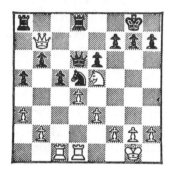

WHITE

Some useful pointers

For White:

1. Play your Queen Rook fairly early to Queen Bishop 1 with a view to controlling the Queen Bishop file. Many of White's most notable wins with this opening have been scored with the help of this technique.

2. Strive to plant your Knight at King 5. Here the Knight is a tower of strength and radiates power in all directions.

3. Your King Bishop belongs on the attacking diagonal Queen Knight 1–King Rook 7, leading right to Black's castled position. (You get the desired effect by playing B–Q3 in the opening.) A concentrated attack by this Bishop and White's Queen—sometimes with the aid of a Rook—has often led to a brilliant and effective finish.

4. Avoid excessive simplifying exchanges. As you have a greater command of the board, simplifying exchanges will only

dilute your greater mobility and make it that much easier for Black to equalize.

For Black:

1. Concentrate on freeing your Queen Bishop. This, as you have seen, is always your basic problem in this opening. You can seek this freedom by preparing to play the Bishop to Queen Knight 2, or by opening his original diagonal with . . . P–K4. In either case, this liberating maneuver calls for careful preparation.

2. Avoid weakening Pawn moves on the King-side—such moves as . . . P–KN3 or . . . P–KR3. Such weaknesses form convenient targets for the enemy's attack. Often such an attack will triumph by means of sacrifices that exploit the weaknesses created by the offending Pawn moves.

3. Be careful not to create a "hole" at your King 4 square. This is explained in the discussion of Diagram 7 in this chapter.

Conclusions

Theoretically this defense seems good enough to draw. However, it is very difficult to conduct in over-the-board play, as we have seen from the two Illustrative Games. The requirements for alertness, patience, and endurance are probably more than we have a right to expect from the average player. We can therefore justifiably conclude that he is better off with the Nimzoindian Defense (Lesson 8), or Gruenfeld Defense (Lesson 9), which are treated later on.

COLLE SYSTEM

WHITE	BLACK
1 P–Q4	P–Q4
2 N–KB3	N–KB3
3 P–K3	P–K3
4 B–Q3	P–B4
5 P–B3	N–B3
6 QN–Q2	B–K2

This deceptively demure opening, named for a famous master who popularized it, can lead to a vicious attack. It was particularly fashionable in the 1930's. Later on the masters found various ways to evade it or draw its sting.

(See Diagram 1)

These moves—and their sequence—should not be accepted in an absolutely rigid fashion. There can be many transpositions in the order of the moves. For example, the game might start off with White playing 1 P–Q4 and Black replying 1 . . . N–KB3. Or White might play out his Queen Knight before developing his King Bishop.

Secondly, Black has some leeway in the development of his Queen Knight and his King Bishop. He can choose between . . . N–QB3 and . . . QN–Q2; similarly, he has a choice between . . . B–K2 and . . . B–Q3. These differences may seem slight. Actually, as you will discover later on, they are of considerable importance.

Position after 6 . . . B–K2
Characteristic position in the Colle System

Diagram 1

BLACK

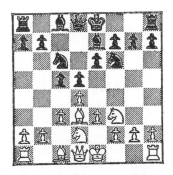

WHITE

A modern device

In modern chess there has been a very marked tendency to play Black defenses with the White side. The reason for this mysterious-seeming trend is that the extra move makes a substantial difference to the value of the opening system.

Since White starts the game, there is a small but persistent probability that he will be more likely to complete his development more rapidly than Black will. Repeatedly we find that Black is just a move short of achieving his Normal Formation at a time when White has completed his task. To make the situation even more critical, the missing move may be the very one that Black needs to obtain equality.

We have a very good example of this in the Orthodox Defense to the Queen's Gambit Declined (Lesson 6). In that line we find Black working very hard to prepare for the crucial equalizing move . . . P–K4. So, the reasoning runs, why not adopt the same formation for White, making use of the extra move to achieve P–K4 fairly effortlessly? Here we have the underlying idea of the Colle System.

It is enlightening to compare the Normal Pawn Skeletons of these two openings:

Queen's Gambit Declined: Orthodox Defense
Normal Pawn Skeleton

Diagram 2

BLACK

WHITE

In Diagram 2, as already pointed out, Black has to work hard for the freeing move . . . P–K4. But now consider the same Pawn formation with the White pieces:

(See Diagram 3)

In the Colle System, as we shall soon see, it is rather easy for White to enforce an early P–K4. This gives him a quick initiative, enables him to develop his Queen Bishop quickly, and often provides the makings of a formidable attack.

Colle System
Normal Pawn Skeleton

Diagram 3

BLACK

WHITE

Elasticity of the Colle System

The heart of White's attacking formation (Diagram 1) is the Bishop at Queen 3 aiming at Black's castled position. The King-side attack might be called White's Maximum Objective, for he has another broad plan available.

In Diagram 4 we see the characteristic Bishop sacrifice which Colle made famous. As a matter of fact, this sacrificial turn is shown in the first Illustrative Game.

However, White is not limited to flashy middle-game attack. He also has fine prospects for the endgame, thanks to the Queen-side majority of Pawns which he develops in the standard variation. White's possession of three Pawns to Black's two on the Queen-side (Diagram 13 in the second Illustrative Game) is a valuable endgame advantage.

Colle System
White's Maximum Objective

Diagram 4

BLACK

WHITE

Colle System
White's Minimum Objective

Diagram 5

BLACK

WHITE

White's attempt to exploit his Queen-side majority of Pawns is his Minimum Objective. Many of the problems connected with this process have been explained in Lesson 4.

The normal course of the variation

In order to familiarize the reader with some of the basic ideas, we will run through the opening moves briefly.

WHITE	BLACK
1 P–Q4	P–Q4
2 N–KB3	N–KB3
3 P–K3	. . .

This move should not be played unthinkingly. It opens up the diagonal of White's King Bishop but closes the diagonal of his other Bishop. White must therefore concentrate on playing P–K4 fairly soon in order to free his imprisoned Queen Bishop.

| 3 . . . | P–K3 |

Black's 3 . . . P–K3 has the virtue of opening up the diagonal of his King Bishop. Yet the move is nothing but thoughtless imitation. Black is likewise limiting his Queen Bishop, but in this case it will not be so easy to obtain freedom. In addition, Black runs the danger of drifting into a passive formation which will leave him ill equipped to counter a brisk attack.

For all these reasons many masters prefer 3 . . . P–KN3 or 3 . . . B–B4. After 3 . . . P–KN3 Black can continue . . . B–N2, developing his game comfortably and secure in the knowledge that the splendid attacking diagonal of White's King Bishop is no longer available.

Of course 3 . . . B–B4 is an even more drastic solution of the problem. Black at once disputes the critical diagonal and thus renders White's B–Q3 perfectly harmless.

| 4 B–Q3 | . . . |

White at once seizes the opportunity which has been presented

Diagram 6

BLACK

WHITE

to him. He now has good attacking chances (after Black has castled) and he is on the way to playing P–K4.

        4 . . .   P–B4

Black makes a flank attack on White's Pawn center.

        5 P–B3   . . .

White supports his Queen Pawn as a preparation for the eventual P–K4. He also creates a haven at Queen Bishop 2 for his King Bishop in the event that this piece is attacked by . . . P–B5. The retreat to Queen Bishop 2 would then keep the King Bishop on his splendid attacking diagonal.

        5 . . .   N–B3

Another way is 5 . . . QN–Q2.

        6 QN–Q2   . . .

This developing move completes White's preparations for P–K4.

        6 . . .   B–K2

Black can also play 6 . . . B–Q3. In that case he can also look forward to playing . . . P–K4 later on.

Position after 6 . . . B–K2
Characteristic position of the Colle System

Diagram 7

BLACK

WHITE

White will now castle and play P–K4, opening up the position advantageously.

White's Normal Formation

White's *King Rook Pawn, King Knight Pawn,* and *King Bishop Pawn* will remain unmoved, as they have nothing to contribute to White's plan of action.

White's *King Pawn* plays to King 3 early in the opening. With proper play on his part, he will be able to advance P–K4 about the eighth move or so, furthering his development and taking the first step toward fashioning a durable King-side attack.

White's *Queen Pawn* plays to Queen 4 on the first move. In

the event that Black plays . . . QBPxQP after White's P–K4, White has a choice of recapture by QBPxP or KNxQP.

If White recaptures with his QBP he will be left with an isolated Queen Pawn. This is a positional weakness, to be sure, but on the other hand White has possibilities of strongly posting a Knight on King 5 or Queen Bishop 5. He also opens the Queen Bishop file for his Rooks. So on the whole the disadvantages and advantages seem to balance fairly well.

On the other hand, if White answers . . . QBPxQP with KNxQP he loses Pawn control of the important squares King 5 and Queen Bishop 5. But against this we must weigh these worthwhile factors: he avoids the weakness of the isolated Queen Pawn; he centralizes his King Knight at Queen 4; and he preserves the endgame advantage of the Queen-side majority of Pawns.

White's *Queen Bishop Pawn* plays to Queen Bishop 3 to support White's Queen Pawn after . . . P–QB4 and also to create a retreat for White's King Bishop at Queen Bishop 2 in the event of Black's playing . . . P–QB5.

White's *Queen Knight Pawn* and *Queen Rook Pawn* remain unmoved at least for the time being. They may advance once White establishes his Queen-side majority of Pawns, as in the second Illustrative Game.

As for White's pieces:

White's *King Knight* is developed at King Bishop 3 early in the opening. If the game proceeds in a quiet positional vein, this Knight usually lands at White's Queen 4 square (second Illustrative Game). If White forms a vehement attack, the Knight is an important participant at King Knight 5 (first Illustrative Game).

Still one more possibility presents itself to this Knight. Sometimes Black prematurely exchanges his Queen Bishop Pawn for White's Queen Pawn at a time when White is still able to retake with his King Pawn. The result is that White gets a half-open King file for his heavy pieces and a powerful outpost at King 5 for a centralized Knight. Here is a fine example from a game Colle–Schubert (Scarborough, 1928).

White smashes through on the King-side

Diagram 8

BLACK

WHITE

With White to play, the game concluded:

WHITE	BLACK
13 N–N5!	P–B3?
14 Q–R5!	P–KN3

Or 14 . . . PxB/N4; 15 BxPch!, NxB; 16 Q–B7ch, K–R1; 17 N–N6 mate.

15 NxNP!	BPxN
16 NxN	N–B3
17 QxNPch	Q–N2
18 NxRP!	Resigns

For if 18 . . . NxN; 19 BxNch, KxB; 20 Q–R5ch and White picks up the Black Rook. This dashing finish is typical of the brilliant attacks unleashed by White in this opening.

White's *Queen Knight* plays to Queen 2. Here it supports the thrust P–K4. After the exchange . . . QPxKP White replies QNxKP. Landing on King 4 in this manner, White's Queen Knight occupies an important center square, threatens to take part in a coming attack, and opens the diagonal of White's Queen Bishop.

White's *King Bishop*, as we know, goes to Queen 3 to support the advance P–K4 and above to serve as the spearhead of White's projected attack.

White's *Queen Bishop* has a delayed development because its diagonal is blocked for some time. Once White has played P–K4 and his Queen Knight has left Queen 2, the Queen Bishop is ready to be deployed. This usually takes the form of B–KN5— certainly the most aggressive development of this Bishop.

White's *King Rook* generally goes to King 1 to operate on the half-open King file. But in situations where White's King Pawn and Queen Pawn and Black's Queen Pawn and Queen Bishop Pawn have disappeared, it is logical to play this Rook to the open Queen file.

White's *Queen Rook* comes into the game tardily because of the late development of White's Queen Bishop. Where a King-side attack is intended, the White Queen Rook may be worked around to that sector by some such maneuver as QR–Q1–Q3–KR3. In quieter situations the Rook may simply take the open Queen file (see under King Rook); or White may strive to double his Rooks on that file.

White's *Queen* goes to the pivot square King 2, available for action on either wing. This is an admirable post for the Queen if White contemplates a King-side attack.

White's *King* goes to King Knight 1 in the course of castling on the King-side.

Black's Normal Formation

Black's *King Rook Pawn* should never be advanced, as . . . P–KR3 creates a target for White's attack. Here we must notice an important distinction: if White plays P–KR3 he is merely wasting time, for the move cannot serve any useful purpose. However, he will not suffer thereby, as Black is not geared for King-side attack. For Black, on the other hand, . . . P–KR3 will merely play into White's hands and make his chances of success that much more likely.

Black's *King Knight Pawn* should likewise remain on its original square, as its advance leads to a critical weakening of Black's black squares on the King-side.

This applies only to the regular variation, in which Black plays . . . P–K3 on the third move or thereabouts. If Black chooses a totally different developing system based on 3 . . . P–KN3 and 4 . . . B–N2 and the avoidance of . . . P–K3, he achieves a very satisfactory formation.

Black's *King Bishop Pawn* should remain on its home square. After . . . P–KB4 or . . . P–KB3 Black will suffer from a lasting weakness in his Pawn position.

Black's *King Pawn* plays to King 3 on the third move. Later on, if the situation is suitable, Black can make a bold thrust to free himself by playing . . . P–K4. To carry this out he must have his King Bishop on Queen 3—that is what is meant by a "suitable situation."

Black's *Queen Pawn* plays to Queen 4 on the first move. It disappears by getting exchanged for White's King Pawn after White plays P–K4.

Black's *Queen Bishop Pawn* advances to Queen Bishop 4 at a fairly early stage in order to exert pressure on White's Pawn center and also to give Black's pieces more playing space. To play . . . P–B5, as inexperienced players sometimes do, is a strategical blunder; it releases the tension in the center and lends added strength to White's ensuing P–K4.

Black's *Queen Knight Pawn* may remain at Queen Knight 2 (as in the first Illustrative Game), or it may advance to Queen Knight 3 (as in the second Illustrative Game) to make room for the fianchetto of Black's Queen Bishop.

Black's *Queen Rook Pawn* remains at Queen Rook 2.

As for Black's pieces:

Black's *King Knight* goes to King Bishop 3 very early in the opening. After the exchange of Pawns resulting from White's P–K4 White's Knight comes to King 4 and very often the Knights are exchanged. As the King Knight is the best bulwark of a castled position, the disappearance of Black's King Knight is one of the factors favoring the success of White's attack.

Black's *Queen Knight* usually goes to Queen Bishop 3. As it happens, this Knight plays to Queen 2 in both our Illustrative Games. The reasons for this are explained under the heading "The normal course of the variation" and they will be repeated later on.

Black's *King Bishop* goes to King 2 if Black plans a conservative defensive game. The Bishop can play to Queen 3 if Black has well-founded hopes of playing . . . P–K4 in the near future.

Black's *Queen Bishop*, as in Lesson 6, presents some problems. The best solution seems to be . . . P–QN3 followed by . . . B–N2. This seems to imply a previous . . . QN–Q2, so that the Bishop at Queen Knight 2 can bear down unimpeded on the center.

Black can also solve the problem drastically by playing 3 . . . B–B4 instead of 3 . . . P–K3. This frees the Bishop at once but leads to a totally different Normal Formation.

Black's *King Rook* remains at King Bishop 1 after castling. In the event that the center is opened up by Pawn exchanges, this Rook may take up a promising post at Queen 1.

Black's *Queen Rook* is not easy to fit into his development scheme. However, Pawn exchanges may open up the position sufficiently to provide a good square for this Rook at Queen Bishop 1.

Black's *Queen* is much less active than the White Queen. The natural square for the Black Queen seems to be Queen Bishop 2, supporting the possible advance . . . P–K4 and making possible the communication of Black's Rooks.

Black's *King* goes to King Knight 1 in the course of castling. As will be seen from the following game, the Black King is often subjected to a withering attack.

ILLUSTRATIVE GAMES

GAME 1

(offers one of the most brilliant examples of the Colle System)

Nice, 1930

WHITE	BLACK
E. Colle	J. O'Hanlon
1 P–Q4	P–Q4
2 N–KB3	N–KB3
3 P–K3	P–B4
4 P–B3	P–K3
5 B–Q3	B–Q3
6 QN–Q2	QN–Q2
7 Castles	Castles

(See Diagram 9)

The purpose of 6 . . . QN–Q2 would now appear after 8 P–K4, BPxP! and White must submit to an isolated Queen Pawn with 9 BPxP, for if 9 NxP, N–B4! favors Black.

Position after 7 . . . Castles
An opening finesse

Diagram 9

BLACK

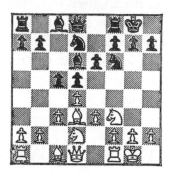

WHITE

8   R–K1!   . . .

Now White is ready for 9 P–K4, for the reply 9 . . . BPxP?
would allow 10 P–K5 winning a piece.

8 . . .   R–K1

Here 8 . . . P–K4 looks plausible, but then 9 P–K4! sets
Black serious difficulties. For example 9 . . . KPxP? loses a piece
to 10 P–K5.

9   P–K4   QPxP
10   NxP   NxN
11   BxN   PxP

Though this move is just barely playable, it leads to serious
trouble. Hence 11 . . . N–B3 was safer.

12   BxPch!!?   . . .

This unexpected sacrifice seems to deprive Black of his wits.
(See Diagram 4.)

12 . . .   KxB
13   N–N5ch   . . .

Note that this attack would have been altogether impossible if Black had played . . . B–K2 instead of . , , B–Q3.

Position after 13 N–N5ch
Where does Black's King go?

Diagram 10

BLACK

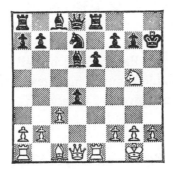

WHITE

At first sight 13 . . . K–N1 seems disastrous for Black because of 14 Q–R5, for example 14 . . . N–B3 (too late!); 15 QxPch, K–R1; 16 R–K4!, NxR; 17 Q–R5ch, K–N1; 18 Q–R7ch, K–B1; 19 Q–R8ch, K–K2; 20 QxP mate.

But after 13 . . . K–N1!; 14 Q–R5, N–K4! White has nothing better than a draw by 15 RxN, BxR; 16 QxPch, K–R1; 17 Q–R5ch White must be content with a perpetual check, for after 17 . . . K–N1 he cannot play 18 Q–R7ch?, K–B1; 19 Q–R8ch, K–K2 and Black's King Knight Pawn is guarded by his Bishop on King 4.

13 . . .   K–N3?

Black does not appreciate the strength of White's reply.

14 P–KR4!! . . .

The chief threat is now 15 P–R5ch, K–R3; 16 NxBP dbl ch winning the Black Queen—or 15 . . . K–B3; 16 Q–B3ch with crushing effect.

There are many interesting possibilities now, all of them bad for Black. For example:

If 14 . . . Q–K2; 15 P–R5ch, K–R3; 16 NxKP dis ch, K–R2; 17 N–N5ch winning Black's Queen.

Or 14 . . . Q–B3; 15 P–R5ch, K–R3; 16 N–K4 dis ch likewise winning Black's Queen.

Or 14 . . . N–B3; 15 Q–Q3ch, K–R4; 16 Q–B3ch, N–N5 (or 16 . . . K–N3; 17 P–R5ch! winning); 17 QxBPch, KxP; 18 N–B3 mate!

Finally, if 14 . . . P–B4; 15 P–R5ch, K–B3; 16 QxPch, B–K4; 17 Q–KR4 and White's numerous threats (such as P–KB4 or B–B4 or N–B3 dis ch) give him an easy win.

Position after 14 P–KR4!!
Black is lost

Diagram 11

BLACK

WHITE

14 . . .   R–R1

This stops P–R5ch—or does it?—but it results in another terrible surprise.

15 RxPch!!   . . .

This Rook is immune from capture, for if 15 . . . PxR; 16 Q–Q3ch, K–B3 (if 16 . . . K–R4; 17 Q–B3ch wins, while if 16 . . . K–R3; 17 NxP dis ch forces the issue); 17 Q–B3ch, B–B5; 18 QxBch, K–K2; 19 Q–B7ch, K–Q3; 20 QxKPch, K–B4 (on 20 . . . K–B2; 21 B–B4ch ends it all); 21 P–N4ch, K–N4; 22 P–R4 mate!

Even 15 . . . P–B3 does not help. There follows 16 P–R5ch!!, RxP; 17 Q–Q3ch, K–R3; 18 Q–R7 mate.

15 . . .   N–B3
16 P–R5ch!   . . .

So White plays this move anyway. The point is that after 16 . . . RxP he has 17 Q–Q3ch, K–R3; 18 Q–R7 mate or 18 NxP mate.

16 . . .   K–R3

Now 17 NxP dis ch wins Black's Queen, but White chooses another way.

17 RxB   Q–R4

If 17 . . . Q–K2; 18 NxP dbl ch, K–R2; 19 N–N5ch, K–R3; 20 N–K4 dis ch, K–R2; 21 NxNch, PxN; 22 Q–Q3ch and wins.

(See Diagram 12)

18 NxP dbl ch K–R2
19 N–N5ch   K–N1

Or 19 . . . K–R3; 20 N–K6 dis ch, K–R2; 21 Q–Q3ch, K–N1; 22 R–Q8ch, K–B2; 23 N–N5ch and White wins.

20 Q–N3ch   Resigns

Black's defenses have been exhausted. A colorful game which gives us a good idea of White's attacking resources.

Position after 17 . . . Q–R4
Black is defenseless

Diagram 12

BLACK

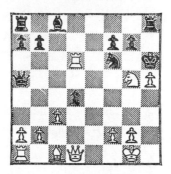

WHITE

GAME 2

(is an example of White's utilization of the Queen-side majority of Pawns)

Pasadena, 1932

WHITE	BLACK
I. Kashdan	*H. Steiner*
1 P–Q4	P–Q4
2 N–KB3	N–KB3
3 P–K3	P–K3
4 B–Q3	QN–Q2
5 QN–Q2	B–K2
6 Q–K2	P–B4
7 P–B3	Castles
8 Castles	P–QN3

Black prepares to fianchetto his Queen Bishop.

9   P–K4   . . .

Black cannot allow P–K5, which would give him an intolerably cramped game.

9	. . .	QPxP
10	NxP	B–N2
11	R–Q1	. . .

A clear indication that White is heading for a purely positional type of game and does not care for a King-side attack.

11	. . .	Q–B2
12	B–KN5	KR–K1
13	PxP	BxN
14	BxB	NxB
15	QxN	NxP
16	Q–QB4	BxB
17	NxB	Q–K2
18	N–B3	. . .

Position after 18 N–B3
White has a positional advantage

Diagram 13

BLACK

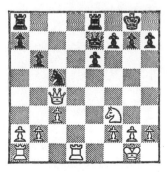

WHITE

White has three Pawns to two on the Queen-side—the famous Queen-side majority of Pawns. If he advances these Pawns systematically he should end up with a distant passed Pawn far away from the Black King.

18 ...　　　KR–Q1
19 N–Q4　　Q–R5

Black threatens . . . P–K4.

20 Q–K2　　QR–B1
21 P–QR4　 ...

Note that 21 P–QN4? would be premature because of 21 . . . N–R5.

21 ...　　　Q–B3
22 P–QN4　N–Q2
23 N–N5　 ...

White does not fear 23 . . . P–QR3; 24 N–Q6, RxP? because of 25 N–K4 winning the Exchange.

23 ...　　　N–B1
24 Q–K3　 ...

By giving his Queen Bishop Pawn extra protection White threatens 25 RxR followed by 26 NxP.

24 ...　　　P–QR3
25 N–Q6　　R–N1

But not 25 . . . RxP?; 26 N–K4, RxQ; 27 NxQch and White comes out the Exchange ahead.

26 R–Q2　　...

White prepares to double Rooks on the open Queen Bishop file; but not 26 P–QB4?, RxN!

26 ...　　　Q–K2
27 QR–Q1　Q–B2
28 P–QB4　 ...

(See Diagram 14)

White's coming P–B5 will be strategically decisive.

28 ...　　　R–Q2

Position after 28 P–QB4
White's Queen-side majority has become menacing

Diagram 14

BLACK

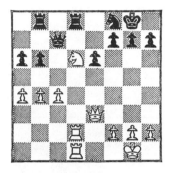

WHITE

29	Q–QB3	P–R3
30	N–K4	. . .

This lends greater force to the coming P–B5 and in addition paves the way for exchanges that will simplify White's technical problems.

30	. . .	RxR
31	RxR	R–B1
32	N–Q6	R–Q1
33	P–B5!	. . .

At last. Here is a likely possibility: 33 . . . PxP; 34 QxP, QxQ; 35 PxQ, R–Q2 (else P–B6 wins at once); 36 P–B6, R–B2; 37 R–B2, N–N3; 38 N–K8, R–B1; 39 P–B7, N–K2; 40 N–Q6 and White wins. A fine example of the utilization of a passed Pawn.

33	. . .	Q–B3
34	Q–B3!	. . .

This requires accurate calculation.

34   . . .   QxRP
35   QxPch   K–R2

Black threatens mate and he has a secondary threat of . . .
QxP.

Position after 35 . . . K–R2
White seems to be hard pressed

Diagram 15

BLACK

WHITE

36   P–R3!   . . .

This lifts the mate threat. Now it turns out that 36 . . .
QxP? loses to 37 N–K4!!, RxR; 38 N–B6ch and mate next move.

36   . . .   PxP

Here, strangely enough, 37 N–K4? would be a mistake because of 37 . . . Q–R8ch; 38 K–R2, RxR and White's check
at King Bishop 6 is covered by the Black Queen.

37   PxP   . . .

This Pawn is now a passed Pawn, but it looks shaky: 37
. . . Q–R8ch; 38 K–R2, Q–K4ch; 39 P–B4, QxQBP? But then
40 N–K4! wins.

	37 . . .	R–N1
	38 K–R2	. . .

Black was now actually threatening to win the Pawn.

	38 . . .	N–N3

This does not really offer the King Pawn, for if 39 QxKP?, Q–KB5ch wins White's Rook.

	39 R–K2	R–KB1

Now White can win a Pawn, but if instead 39 . . . N–B1; 40 N–K4 wins.

40	QxKP	Q–KB5ch
41	P–N3	Q–Q5
42	Q–K3	QxQ
43	PxQ	N–K4

Position after 43 . . . N–K4
White's Queen Bishop Pawn decides the issue

Diagram 16

BLACK

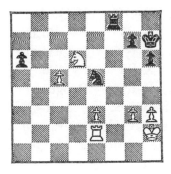

WHITE

44	K–N2	P–QR4

The counterthreat.

45	R–QB2	N–B3
46	N–N5!	. . .

In order to uproot Black's blockading Knight.

46	. . .	R–Q1
47	N–Q4!	NxN
48	PxN	RxP
49	P–B6	R–Q1
50	K–B3!	. . .

But not 50 P–B7?, R–QB1; 51 K–B3, P–R5; 52 K–K4, P–R6; 53 K–Q5, P–R7; 54 RxP, RxP, etc. However, the approach of White's King wins.

50	. . .	P–R5

No better is 50 . . . K–N3; 51 K–K4, K–B3; 52 P–B7, R–QB1; 53 K–Q5, K–K2; 54 K–B6, P–R5; 55 K–N7, K–Q2; 56 R–Q2ch and White wins.

51	K–K4	P–R6
52	K–K5	R–Q6

Black admits defeat. The absence of his King from the critical sector tells against him.

53	P–B7	P–R7
54	RxP	R–QB6
55	K–Q6	R–Q6ch
56	K–B6	R–QB6ch
57	K–N7	R–QN6ch
58	K–R8	R–QB6
59	R–R7	Resigns

For if 59 . . . K–N3; 60 K–N8, R–QN6ch; 61 R–N7 and the Pawn must queen. A splendid example of logical, consistent play in which White transformed his Queen-side majority into a winning passed Pawn.

Some useful pointers

For White:

1. After . . . B–Q3 play for a King-side attack.

2. After . . . B–K2 play to obtain the Queen-side majority of Pawns.

3. Play P–K4 at the earliest suitable opportunity.

4. Play Q–K2 fairly early to establish communication between your Rooks.

For Black:

1. Play your King Bishop to King 2 as the best protection against a strong White King-side attack.

2. Play . . . B–Q3 only if you are sure to be able to follow up with . . . P–K4.

3. Concentrate on the problem of developing your Queen Bishop.

4. Avoid characteristic weakening moves such as . . . P–KR3 or . . . P–KN3.

Conclusions

In a sense this opening is much simpler for White than it is for Black. White has his well-defined Maximum Objective (King-side attack) and Minimum Objective (favorable endgame with the Queen-side Pawn majority). Black, on the other hand, lacks such clear-cut objectives and must take his lead from White. This limits Black to a policy of watchful waiting—a task not to everyone's taste.

This explains why many players have preferred to vary with 3 . . . B–B4 or 3 . . . P–KN3. The resulting play is easier for Black because White's objectives are not presented to him with equal clarity.

NIMZOINDIAN DEFENSE

(4 Q–B2 variation)

WHITE	BLACK
1 P–Q4	N–KB3
2 P–QB4	P–K3
3 N–QB3	B–N5

This defense is suffused with a highly aggressive spirit. The watchword is "counterattack." It has enjoyed tremendous popularity in master play since the early 1920's.

(See Diagram 1)

The name of this defense is actually a compound word that needs some explaining. "Indian" is the term used for defenses in which Black counters 1 P–Q4 with 1 . . . N–KB3 instead of the almost mechanical reply 1 . . . P–Q4. The first part of "Nimzoindian" comes from Aron Nimzovich (1887–1935), a brilliant, profound and somewhat erratic genius who popularized this defense and contributed some of its leading ideas.

Normal course of the variation

WHITE	BLACK
1 P–Q4	N–KB3

This move announces a program. Black naturally wants to restrain White from forming a broad Pawn center with P–K4,

Position after 3 . . . B–N5
The basic position

Diagram 1

BLACK

WHITE

which would have a stifling effect on Black's game. Black can accomplish his aim with the "simple" 1 . . . P–Q4; but, as we have seen in Lesson 6, the consequences of 1 . . . P–Q4 are anything but simple.

By playing 1 . . . N–KB3 Black prevents P–K4 for the time being and gains a respite for deciding how he will prevent P–K4 later on. This gives us an idea of the resourcefulness and elasticity of the defense.

2   P–QB4   . . .

Part of the struggle for the center. The idea is that White can answer 2 . . . P–Q4 with 3 PxP. Then if 3 . . . NxP; 4 P–K4 or 3 . . . QxP; 4 N–QB3. In either case White has a strong grip on the center.

2 . . .   P–K3

A preparation for . . . P–Q4 (if Blacks wants to play it) and also for . . . B–N5, either of these moves being part of the struggle for the center.

3   N–QB3   . . .

Position after 3 N–QB3
White threatens P–K4

Diagram 2

BLACK

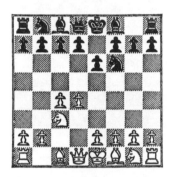

WHITE

White threatens to monopolize the center with P–K4. Black can meet the threat with 3 . . . P–Q4, but instead he chooses an alternative method.

3   . . .   B–N5

By pinning White's Queen Knight, Black prevents 4 P–K4? which would simply be answered by 4 . . . NxP. This illuminates the counterattacking character of the Nimzoindian Defense.

4   Q–B2   . . .

Once more White threatens P–K4. Black has two ways of countering this possibility.

One is to allow P–K4 and immediately take steps to form a countercenter, for example 4 . . . N–B3; 5 N–B3, P–Q3 followed in due course by . . . P–K4. This is a perfectly acceptable line of play.

The other way for Black to proceed—and the one we shall study here—is 4 . . . P–Q4.

4 . . .   P–Q4

5 PxP   QxP

Note that 5 . . . PxP (freeing Black's Queen Bishop) is perfectly playable here. But experience has shown that the move leads to dull, rather drawish play. So Black chooses the more adventurous reply.

6 N–B3   P–B4

Black attacks White's Pawn center from the wing.

Position after 6 . . . P–B4
How should White proceed?

Diagram 3

BLACK

WHITE

White has two main lines of play here:

Variation 1

7 P–QR3   BxNch

Black must exchange, ceding his opponent the two Bishops.

8   PxB   . . .

White hopes to build a strong Pawn center, but his Queen Bishop Pawn may turn out to be weak.

8   . . .   N–B3
9   P–K3   Castles

This line of play is shown in the first Illustrative Game.

Variation 2

7   B–Q2   BxN

Here too Black cedes White the advantage of the two Bishops, as retreating the Queen would be too time-consuming.

8   BxB   PxP
9   NxP   . . .

This line of play is shown in the second Illustrative Game.

Before we proceed to the Normal Formation we need to learn more about the nature and purposes of this defense.

The Orthodox Variation and Nimzoindian Defense compared

In Lesson 6 we saw that the Orthodox Defense to the Queen's Gambit Declined was playable but full of thorny troubles for Black. Chief of these was the difficulty encountered in developing Black's Queen Bishop effectively. In actual practice it frequently happens that Black loses a great deal of time or compromises his position in some manner. The upshot is that he creates weaknesses that invite a winning King-side attack or else leave him with vulnerable points on the Queen-side.

There is a paradoxical aspect of the Orthodox Defense that deserves our notice. Black plays 1 . . . P–Q4, which gives the impression that he means to fight for possession of the center. Yet later on he gives up the center with . . . QPxQBP in order to bring about some simplifying exchanges that will ease his crowded position. Thereafter Black must fight for his fair share of the center.

This is a defect that the Nimzoindian Defense aims to cure or avoid. Black concentrates on fighting for the center, using his pieces rather than Pawns for the purpose.

If the Orthodox Variation typifies passive defense, then the Nimzoindian Defense by the same token stands for energetic counterattack. In carrying out his aim, Black relies on two techniques: he tries to develop rapidly, and he tries to hinder White's Pieces from obtaining too much scope. In Lesson 6, if you recall, White developed pretty much as he pleased, without interference from Black.

Before we go on to a study of the Normal Formation, it will be useful to picture the Normal Pawn Skeleton of Variations 1 and 2.

Variation 1
Normal Pawn Skeleton

Diagram 4a

BLACK

WHITE

Variation 2
Normal Pawn Skeleton

Diagram 4b

BLACK

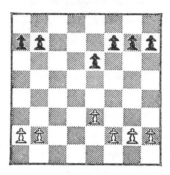

WHITE

White's Normal Formation

White's *King Rook Pawn, King Knight Pawn,* and *King Bishop Pawn* all remain unmoved.

White's *King Pawn* plays to King 3 to support the Queen Pawn and to prepare for the development of White's King Bishop.

When White has Pawns on Queen Bishop 3, Queen 4, and King 3 and Black has a Pawn on his Queen Bishop 4, Black often plays . . . QBPxQP. In that case White may retake with the King Pawn, though this has the drawback of leaving his Queen Bishop Pawn exposed to attack on the half-open Queen Bishop file. This is drastically indicated in the first Illustrative Game.

White's *Queen Pawn* advances to Queen 4 on the first move. It is usually the Queen Pawn's fate to be exchanged for Black's Queen Bishop Pawn.

White's *Queen Bishop Pawn* is exchanged at a very early stage for Black's Queen Pawn.

White's *Queen Knight Pawn* recaptures on Queen Bishop 3 after . . . BxNch in Variation 1. This Pawn may become a serious weakness, as the first Illustrative Game shows. To return to the situation of Diagram 4a, if Black plays . . . QBPxQP, White also has the alternative of recapturing with his Queen Bishop Pawn. This rids him of a potential weakness, but it is not wholly without drawbacks. For Black is likely to be the first to get to the open Queen Bishop file; and in addition he has a potential endgame advantage in his Queen-side majority of Pawns.

White's *Queen Rook Pawn* plays to Queen Rook 3 in Variation 1 to force . . . BxNch. This is an important point, as White pins his faith to the possession of the two Bishops against Bishop and Knight. However, this hope may play him false.

As for White's pieces:

White's *King Knight* plays to King Bishop 3, where it has its usual role of exerting pressure on White's King 5 square and guarding White's Queen Pawn.

White's *Queen Knight* plays to Queen Bishop 3 on the third move and is exchanged for Black's King Bishop at an early stage.

White's *King Bishop* plays to King 2 or Queen 3. The King 2 development is called for in a positional game, whereas White may try B–Q3 in a situation where he has aggressive prospects involving an attempt to play P–K4.

White's *Queen Bishop* has poor prospects in Variation 1, for the White Pawn complex Queen Bishop 3, Queen 4, and King 3 does not allow this Bishop much scope. The future of this Bishop brightens somewhat in the event of an exchange of White's Queen Pawn or the disappearance of White's Pawn at Queen

Bishop 3. Generally speaking, the two Bishops are not a formidable weapon in this variation.

In Variation 2, where White's Queen Bishop reaches Queen Bishop 3 very quickly, the Bishop has a fine diagonal. This is the variation in which White's Bishops are likely to play an important role.

White's *Rooks* have this choice: in Variation 1 King Rook on King square (after KPxQP) and Queen Rook on Queen Bishop file. This is not a particularly effective setup.

In Variation 2 White's Rooks will play as follows: King Rook to the Queen file, Queen Rook to the Queen Bishop file. In this variation the Rooks are well placed on the open files and ready to operate effectively.

White's *Queen* goes to Queen Bishop 2 on the fourth move. In Variation 1, as shown in the first Illustrative Game, White's Queen is none too happy here. In Variation 2 (second Illustrative Game), on the other hand, the Queen plays an effective role.

White's *King* goes to King Knight 1 in the course of castling.

Black's Normal Formation

Black's *King Rook Pawn, King Knight Pawn,* and *King Bishop Pawn* should remain on their initial squares.

Black's *King Pawn* plays to King 3 on the second move. In Variation 2 (second Illustrative Game) it is generally able to advance to King 4.

Black's *Queen Pawn* goes to Queen 4. It is soon exchanged for White's Queen Bishop Pawn.

Black's *Queen Bishop Pawn* strikes at White's center by . . . P–QB4. In Variation 1 (first Illustrative Game) this thrust is extremely inconvenient for White, as it is bound to uncover some weakness in his game. Either he is left with a weak Queen Bishop Pawn or else he is exposed to pressure along the Queen Bishop file.

Black's *Queen Knight Pawn* plays to Queen Knight 3 in Variation 1 to allow for the development of Black's Queen Bishop to Queen Knight 2 (sometimes to Queen Rook 3). In contrast to the Orthodox Variation, this Bishop is developed without the slightest trouble and is soon able to function effectively.

Black's *Queen Rook Pawn* remains on its home square.

As for Black's pieces:

Black's *King Bishop* is developed to Queen Knight 5 on the third move and is presently exchanged for White's Queen Knight. This exchange is absolutely essential if Black is to maintain himself in the center and avoid a grievous loss of time.

Black's *Queen Bishop* is developed at Queen Knight 2 in Variation 1. In Variation 2, however, Black is generally able to advance . . . P–K4, which means that he will be able to develop this Bishop on his original diagonal.

Black's *King Knight* plays to King Bishop 3 on the first move, immediately starting the struggle for control of Black's vital King 5 square.

Black's *Queen Knight* goes to Queen Bishop 3. In Variation 1 it will later play to Queen Rook 4 as part of Black's pressure on the Queen Bishop file. In Variation 2 it will support the advance . . . P–K4.

Black's *Queen Rook* plays to the Queen Bishop file, where it is particularly effective in Variation 1.

Black's *King Rook* goes to the Queen file. When this file is completely open, the Rook will dispute any attempt by White to control the file.

Black's *Queen* takes up a strongly centralized post at Black's Queen 4 square after White plays QBPxQP. As in all cases when a Queen is centralized, a number of useful opportunities will open up during the game.

Black's *King* goes to King Knight 1 in the course of castling.

ILLUSTRATIVE GAMES

GAME 1

(shows how Black utilizes his prospects on the Queen Bishop file in Variation 1)

Berne, 1932

WHITE	BLACK
A. Staehelin	A. Alekhine
1 P–Q4	N–KB3
2 P–QB4	P–K3
3 N–QB3	B–N5
4 Q–B2	P–Q4
5 PxP	QxP
6 N–B3	P–B4
7 P–QR3	. . .

Forcing the following exchange of Bishop for Knight, but 7 B–Q2 (developing, and avoiding Pawn weaknesses) is the recommended move.

| 7 . . . | BxNch |
| 8 PxB | . . . |

After 8 QxB, N–K5 Black has the initiative by reason of his powerful grip on his King 5 square.

| 8 . . . | N–B3 |
| 9 P–K3 | Castles |

White's Pawn complex at Queen Bishop 3, Queen 4, and King 3 spells trouble for White as soon as Black completes his preparations for operating on the Queen Bishop file.

Another prospective difficulty is this: with so many White Pawns on black squares, the mobility of White's Queen Bishop is seriously reduced. This explains why White's Bishop-pair—ordinarily a notable positional advantage—is of no great moment here.

Position after 9 . . . Castles
Storm warning for White

Diagram 5

BLACK

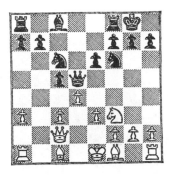

WHITE

10	B–K2	P–QN3
11	Castles	PxP!

To this White's relatively best reply was 12 BPxP, getting rid of a potential weakness; although after 12 . . . B–N2; 13 B–N2, QR–B1 Black is already threatening . . . NxP, thereby forcing White's Queen to get off the Queen Bishop file.

Another weighty point is that after 12 BPxP Black would have an additional positional advantage in his Queen-side majority of Pawns. This explains why White avoids 12 BPxP. Yet that was his best chance.

12	KPxP?	B–N2

The weakness of White's Pawn formation is already manifest. This explains White's next move, played to give his Queen Pawn additional protection in the event of P–B4.

13	R–Q1	QR–B1!

Playing with admirable simplicity, Black is already well ahead in development and is now ready to continue with . . . N–QR4–B5.

Position after 13 . . . *QR–B1!*
White is in trouble

Diagram 6

BLACK

WHITE

14   P–B4   . . .

A very natural move, played to forestall the coming . . . N–QR4–B5. But Black has a reply as effective as it is surprising.

14 . . .   N–QR4!

This wins a Pawn in some instances, for example 15 PxQ, RxQ; 16 B–Q3 (apparently saving everything), N–N6!; 17 BxR (or 17 R–N1, RxB and Black still winds up a Pawn ahead), NxR; 18 B–R4, BxP after which Black's wandering Knight escapes, leaving him a Pawn to the good.

15   Q–R4   NxP

Now White is in a quandary. If he plays 16 BxN, QxB; 17 QxP he gets a hopeless game after 17 . . . BxN!; 18 PxB, N–Q4! when Black threatens . . . R–B2 (winning White's Queen—not to mention . . . Q–K7, which wins at least a Pawn).

16   R–N1   . . .

Equivalent to surrender.

16   . . .   P–QR3

Preparing to reinforce his Knight with . . . P–QN4. The reply
17 BxN is worthless because of 17 . . . RxB followed by 18 . . .
P–QN4.

17   N–K1   P–QN4
18   Q–N3   Q–KB4
19   B–Q3   B–K5!
20   BxB?   . . .

This loses, although after 20 P–B3, BxB; 21 NxB, N–Q4 Black
would have a won game anyway.

20   . . .   NxB

Black threatens mate in two.

21   P–B3   . . .

White parries the threat but allows Black to win in a different
way.

Position after 21 P–B3
Black wins material

Diagram 7

BLACK

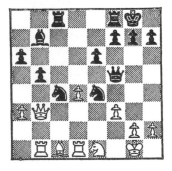

WHITE

One would expect Black's Knight to retreat. Instead:

21 . . .   N–B6!

Resigns

White must lose the exchange, for example 22 QxN/B3, QxR. As this would leave Black with a substantial material advantage, White prefers to give up the unequal struggle.

GAME 2

(is a convincing example of the superiority of Variation 2 from White's point of view)

Amsterdam, 1938

WHITE	BLACK
J. R. Capablanca	*M. Euwe*
1 P–Q4	N–KB3
2 P–QB4	P–K3
3 N–QB3	B–N5
4 Q–B2	P–Q4
5 PxP	QxP
6 N–B3	P–B4
7 B–Q2!	. . .

Superior to 7 P–QR3, which White played in the previous game.

7 . . .	BxN
8 BxB	PxP
9 NxP	P–K4

(See Diagram 8)

10 N–B5   . . .

Practically forcing the following exchange, for if Black protects his attacked King Knight Pawn by castling, White replies 11 N–K7ch, winning Black's Queen.

Position after 9 . . . P–K4
Black obtains freedom—at a price

Diagram 8

BLACK

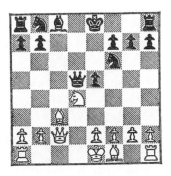

WHITE

10	. . .	BxN
11	QxB	N–B3

Black's freedom of action and his lead in development compensate to some extent for White's two Bishops.

12	P–K3	Castles (K)
13	B–K2!	. . .

Giving Black the opportunity to play 13 . . . QxNP, for after 14 B–B3, Q–N3; 15 QxQ, RPxQ; 16 BxN, PxB; 17 BxP White has a very superior ending, thanks to Black's irremediably weak Queen Bishop Pawn and his weakness on the black squares.

13	. . .	Q–K5
14	Q–B3	. . .

Naturally White is averse to 14 QxQ, NxQ, after which he cannot preserve his Queen Bishop.

14	. . .	Q–B7?

In the event, this turns out to be sheer loss of time. The proper course was . . . KR–K1 in conjunction with . . . QR–Q1.

Position after 14 . . . Q–B7?
Black sets a foolish trap

Diagram 9

BLACK

WHITE

Black is under the impression that White must not castle because of 15 . . . P–K5 winning White's King Bishop.

       15   Castles!   QR–Q1

For after 15 . . . P–K5; 16 Q–N3, QxB/K7; 17 BxN and White wins easily. However, 15 . . . P–QR3 was better than Black's Rook move.

       16   B–N5!   R–Q4

The only way to prevent immediate loss of a Pawn.

       17   QR–B1   Q–K5
       18   Q–K2   . . .

Black's position is worse than it looks. Consider, for example, the following intricate line of play: 18 . . . R–B1; 19 P–B3, Q–N3; 20 P–K4, R–B4; 21 P–QN4, N–Q5; 22 Q–Q3!, RxB/B6; 23 RxR, N–K7ch (not 23 . . . RxR; 24 QxR, NxB; 25 Q–B8ch and mate next move); 24 QxN, RxR; 25 Q–N2 and White wins a Pawn.

       18   . . .   R–Q3

19 P–B3   Q–B4
20 BxN!   RxB

And not 20 . . . PxB; 21 D–N4 when White wins the exchange.

Position after 20 . . . RxB
Now White wins a Pawn

Diagram 10

BLACK

WHITE

21 Q–N5!   KR–B1

This prevents 22 QxKP? which would lose a Rook.

22 QxNP   Q–Q6
23 P–K4   . . .

Here Black has a gallant try with 23 . . . Q–K6ch; 24 K–R1, N–R4 (threatening . . . N–N6ch and mate next move); 25 QxRch!, RxQ; 26 B–Q2! RxR; 27 RxR and is lost because of White's mate threat.

23 . . .   N–R4
24 P–KN3!   . . .

More prudent than 24 QxRP, N–B5 when Black has some counterchances.

		Q–K6ch
24	. . .	Q–K6ch
25	K–N2	Q–N4
26	K–B2	P–B4

Desperate because of his material disadvantage, Black gives up a piece to trouble the muddied waters.

27	PxP	QxBP
28	P–KN4	Q–B5
29	PxN	QxRPch
30	K–K3	Q–B5ch
31	K–K2	Q–B5ch
32	K–K1	Q–Q6
33	Q–N3ch	. . .

Now White consolidates his position.

33	. . .	K–R1
34	R–QB2!	R–B3
35	R–Q2	Q–B4
36	Q–B2	Q–B5
37	Q–K4	Q–N6ch
38	R/B1–B2	Q–N8ch
39	K–K2	R/B3–B1
40	P–R6!	Resigns

And rightly so. If 40 . . . PxP; 41 QxKPch, K–N1; 42 Q–K6ch! is murderous.

Some useful pointers

For White:

1. Avoid Variation 1, as White is at a disadvantage with his ineffectual Queen Bishop. What makes matters even worse for him is Black's pressure on the Queen Bishop file.

2. Strive for Variation 2, which gives White a promising two-Bishop game.

3. Try to keep control of the important King 4 square at all times.

4. Be sure to place your Rooks on the open files.

For Black:

1. Try to keep the Queen at its centralized post at Queen 4 as long as possible.

2. In Variation 1 play the Queen Bishop to Queen Knight 2; in Variation 2, advance . . . P–K4 to develop the Bishop on its original diagonal.

3. However, be chary of a premature . . . P–K4 which may open up the game effectively for White's bishops.

4. Since you will be left with Bishop and Knight against two Bishops—or perhaps even two Knights against two Bishops—you must be alert for opportunities to keep your pieces in good play.

Conclusions

Black undoubtedly gets a good game both from the theoretical and the practical view. White does badly with 7–QR3 (Variation 1). He is much better off with 7 B–Q2 (Variation 2).

As we have seen, Black has to play alertly to hold his own in Variation 2. But on balance he has a much more promising game than in the Orthodox Variation; he is active rather than passive, and he has a variety of possibilities at his disposal. Black should therefore prefer this defense to the Orthodox Variation.

Lesson 9

GRUENFELD DEFENSE

(4 PxP Variation)

WHITE	BLACK
1 P–Q4	N–KB3
2 P–QB4	P–KN3
3 N–QB3	P–Q4

Position after 3 . . . P–Q4
The basic position

Diagram 1

BLACK

WHITE

Starting with 1 . . . N–KB3, this is an "Indian" defense. But
with 3 . . . P–Q4 Black seems to return to an orthodox forma-

tion after all. The effect is, however, to allow White to establish
a very powerful-looking Pawn center. Black's job is to attack this
Pawn center from the wings. This is known as "hypermodern"
strategy.

White has many replies to choose from, for example 4 PxP or
4 P–K3 or 4 B–B4 or 4 Q–N3. We are selecting 4 PxP because
it is the most obvious move and also the one that leads to the
most critical play.

4   PxP   NxP

Now Black has no Pawn foothold in the center, and according
to old-fashioned conceptions he must be very badly off.

5   P–K4   . . .

White immediately establishes a powerful-looking Pawn center.

5   . . .   NxN
6   PxN   . . .

Better and better, says White. Now his Queen Pawn has
gained strong support.

6   . . .   P–QB4!

But this puts a somewhat different complexion on the matter.
Black attacks White's Pawn center from the flank. If White
pushes by (7 P–Q5), Black plays 7 . . . B–N2 with a magnificent
diagonal for his fianchettoed Bishop.

If White tries 7 PxP, Black gets a fine game with 7 . . .
QxQch; 8 KxQ, B–N2; 9 B–Q2, B–K3, etc. Black recovers the
Pawn at his leisure while he improves his splendid development.
Ultimately he will operate against White's weak and isolated
Pawn at Queen Bishop 3. So 7 PxP is really out of the question.

The only logical course, then, is for White to keep his Queen
Pawn at Queen 4 and strengthen it against the pressure being
exerted by Black.

Position after 6 . . . P–QB4!
White's Pawn center is under attack

Diagram 2

BLACK

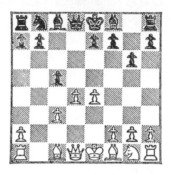

WHITE

Two types of center control

In the previous lesson we touched on the two ways of controlling the center—by occupying it with Pawns or by exerting pressure on it with pieces.

The first type calls for a "Classical" center; the second type is known as "Hypermodern" control of the center.

In this variation White, with his Pawns at King 4 and Queen 4, has a classical center. At first sight this Pawn center seems all powerful. But soon we observe that this center is the target of a flank attack (. . . P–QB4) as well as direct attacks on the long diagonal (. . . B–KN2) and on the Queen file (say . . . Q–Q2 and . . . KR–Q1). By means of these counterattacks Black is exerting pressure on the center. That is what we mean by hypermodern control.

This state of affairs confers a further theoretical advantage on White: he has a tangible object of attack. From this point of view the "powerful" Pawn center may turn out to be a distinct liability for White.

Normal Pawn Skeleton
Before the Pawn exchange

Diagram 3a

BLACK

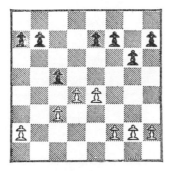

WHITE

White's Normal Formation

White's *King Rook Pawn* and *King Knight Pawn* remain unmoved.

White's *King Bishop Pawn* advances to King Bishop 4 and possibly King Bishop 5 in situations where White has direct attacking chances. (White's King Knight goes to King 2 to clear the way for the advance of the King Bishop Pawn.)

White's *King Pawn* plays to King 4 early in the opening. This Pawn may advance to King 5 as part of a general attack. However, this advance must be judged with great care: it reduces Black's fianchettoed King Bishop to inactivity, but on the other hand it may weaken White's position, and it allows Black to

Normal Pawn Skeleton
After the Pawn exchange

Diagram 3b

BLACK

WHITE

establish his pieces on his Queen 4 square without any danger that they will be driven away.

White's *Queen Pawn* plays to Queen 4 on the first move and becomes the target for Black's counterplay. In some cases White may advance the Queen Pawn to Queen 5, allowing Black to win the exchange by playing . . . BxR along the long diagonal. This speculative sacrifice of the exchange, which appears in the second Illustrative Game, can yield White a very powerful attack.

White's *Queen Bishop Pawn* disappears on the fourth move when it is exchanged for Black's Queen Pawn. This exchange is the preliminary that enables White to set up his broad Pawn center.

White's *Queen Knight Pawn* disappears in the opening when White replies 5 NPxN in reply to Black's 4 . . . NxN. This exchange gives White the open Queen Knight file, which may turn out to be useful later on.

White's *Queen Rook Pawn* remains at Queen Rook 2. Being isolated after the recapture just mentioned, the Pawn may become a serious weakness in the endgame.

As for White's pieces:

White's *King Knight* goes to King 2 (after he has developed his King Bishop, of course). There are a number of reasons why White varies from the more familiar N–KB3. In the first place, the Knight's primary function is to protect the Queen Pawn. But at King Bishop 3 the Knight can be pinned by Black's Queen Bishop (. . . B–KN5), so that the pin operates as an indirect menace against White's Queen Pawn. Hence White plays the King Knight to King 2.

The other reason for this development, as we have seen, is to make room for the advance of White's King Bishop Pawn.

White's *Queen Knight* plays to Queen Bishop 3 on the third move and is soon exchanged for Black's King Knight.

White's *King Bishop* is best posted at Queen Bishop 4, where it aims aggressively at Black's castled position. The Bishop is particularly effective at Queen Bishop 4 when White can open the King Bishop file by playing P–KB4–5.

White's *Queen Bishop* has several possibilities. Its usual development is to King 3, where it stands guard over White's Queen Pawn. However, it is sometimes played to Queen Rook 3 where it commands a fine diagonal. However, the latter development presupposes that White's Queen Pawn is adequately guarded without the help of his Queen Bishop.

White's *Queen Rook* often plays to the Queen Bishop file after it has been opened by Black's playing . . . QBPxQP and White's replying QBPxQP. In that case a struggle for control of the open file might be touched off. The likely result would be the exchange of all four Rooks.

White's *King Rook* stays on King Bishop 1 when he has a good King-side attack. If the game has a predominantly positional cast or if White is on the defensive, his King Rook will go to Queen 1.

If White is attacking, then, his Rooks are likely to be at King Bishop 1 and King 1, or perhaps King Bishop 1 and Queen 1. If White is not intent on attack, then his Rooks will probably be at Queen 1 and Queen Bishop 1.

White's *Queen* generally plays to Queen 2. This facilitates communication between the White Rooks and also makes room for KR–Q1. When White sacrifices the exchange (see the discussion of White's Queen Pawn), the Queen reaches Queen Rook 1 with a vicious attack along the long diagonal.

White's *King* goes to King Knight 1 in the course of castling.

Black's Normal Formation

Black's *King Rook Pawn* stays on its original square.

Black's *King Knight Pawn* plays to King Knight 3 in order to make room for the fianchetto of Black's King Bishop.

Black's *King Bishop Pawn* and *King Pawn* generally remain unmoved.

Black's *Queen Pawn* moves to Queen 4 on the third move and is then exchanged for White's Queen Bishop Pawn.

Black's *Queen Bishop Pawn* moves to Queen Bishop 4 at an early stage in order to put White's Queen Pawn under pressure.

Black's *Queen Knight Pawn* and *Queen Rook Pawn* do not move during the opening. Yet, as we see from Diagram 3b and the first Illustrative Game, these Pawns can become extremely important once Black has played . . . QBPxQP and White has replied QBPxQP. For in that case Black has the celebrated Queen-side majority of Pawns (two to one). This theoretical advantage is often the key to Black's victory in the Gruenfeld Defense. (See the first Illustrative Game.)

As for Black's pieces:

Black's *King Knight* plays to King Bishop 3 on his first move, then to Queen 4 and is then exchanged for White's Queen Knight. One effect of the Knight's early disappearance is that Black's King Bishop has an open diagonal.

Black's *Queen Knight* plays to Queen Bishop 3. Here it has the valuable function of attacking White's Queen Pawn. During the middle game this Knight often plays to Queen Bishop 5 (via Queen Rook 4) as an effective outpost on the open Queen Bishop file. This maneuver is particularly strong in situations where White's King Bishop has been exchanged.

Black's *King Bishop* plays to King Knight 2 in the opening. Its attack on White's Queen Pawn and its operations along the diagonal in general make up the chief theme of Black's play in this opening.

Black's *Queen Bishop* has a less clearly defined role. Sometimes when the opportunity offers, it plays to King Knight 5, pinning White's King Knight and thus indirectly menacing his Queen Pawn. Sometimes when Black is in control of the Queen Bishop file he plays . . . B–K3–QB5, offering the exchange of Bishops. Finally, if nothing better offers, Black can play . . . P–QN3 and . . . B–QN2.

Black's *King Rook* generally plays to Queen 1 to strengthen the pressure on White's Queen Pawn.

Black's *Queen Rook* generally plays to Queen Bishop 1 in the hope of gaining control of the open file or with a view to supporting . . . N–QR4–QB5 or . . . B–K3–QB5.

Black's *Queen* plays to Queen 2 as a rule—or perhaps Queen Bishop 2. Its main function, strangely enough, is to keep out of the way of Black's forces when they exert pressure on White's Queen Pawn. The explanation of the Black Queen's paradoxical inactivity is that Black cannot very well employ his most important piece as the spearhead of an attack on a mere Pawn.

Black's *King* goes to King Knight 1 in the course of castling.

ILLUSTRATIVE GAMES

GAME 1

(shows the value of Black's Queen-side Pawn majority against colorless play)

Vienna, 1923

WHITE	BLACK
J. *von Patay*	R. *Reti*
1 P–Q4	N–KB3
2 P–QB4	P–KN3
3 N–QB3	P–Q4
4 PxP	NxP
5 P–K4	NxN
6 PxN	P–QB4!
7 B–QN5ch	. . .

This feeble move merely simplifies without gaining anything for White after the following exchange. Correct is B–QB4 followed by N–K2.

7 . . .	B–Q2
8 BxBch	QxB
9 N–B3	B–N2

(*See Diagram 4*)

The fact that Black is already ahead in development is a clear sign that White has played weakly. And the coming phase is equally unpromising for White. He has no goal, whereas Black can comfortably concentrate on the Queen Pawn.

10 Castles	PxP
11 PxP	N–B3

Position after 9 . . . B–N2
Black is ahead in development

Diagram 4

BLACK

WHITE

Black's game plays itself.

        12   B–N2   . . .

This makes matters worse: the Bishop is now confined to purely passive tasks. 12 B–K3 is preferable by far.

        12   . . .   Castles (K)
        13   Q–R4   KR–Q1
        14   QR–Q1   N–K4!
        15   QxQ   . . .

White mistakenly seeks safety in simplification. Much better is 15 Q–N3, as the coming endgame is decidedly in Black's favor because of his Queen-side Pawn majority.

        15   . . .   NxNch
        16   PxN   RxQ

(See Diagram 5)

The endgame favors Black for these reasons:

1. He has pressure on White's Queen Pawn.

Position after 16 . . . *RxQ*
A favorable ending for Black

Diagram 5

BLACK

WHITE

2. Black has the Queen-side majority of Pawns, which should normally result in an outside passed Pawn for him.

3. White's Pawn majority is worthless because his King Bishop Pawn is doubled and he has no chance of creating a passed Pawn.

Consider this possibility: 17 R–Q2, R–QB1; 18 KR–Q1, B–R3; 19 R–K2, R/Q2–B2 followed by . . . R–B7 and Black should win the ending in due course by bringing his King to Queen-side.

Or 17 P–K5, P–B3! leaving White these choices:

1. 18 PxP, BxP and White's Queen Pawn, being isolated, is a more vulnerable target than ever before.

2. 18 P–K6, R–Q3; 19 KR–K1, P–B4 and White will soon lose a Pawn.

3. 18 P–B4, B–R3; 19 B–B1, R–QB1 and Black occupies the seventh rank with a strategically won game.

4. 18 KR–K1, QR–Q1 and Black maintains powerful pressure.

17   R–Q3   R–QB1

Gaining control of the all-important file. White cannot fight back with 18 R–B1, as that would lose a Pawn.

18   KR–Q1   R–B7

19   R/Q1–Q2 R/Q2–B2

20   P–QR3   . . .

Position after 20 P–QR3
Black makes important headway

Diagram 6

BLACK

WHITE

20   . . .   B–R3!

This nails down Black's control of the seventh rank.

21   RxR   RxR

22   B–B3   . . .

Or 22 R–N3, P–N3; 23 P–Q5, B–B5 with considerable advantage for Black.

22   . . .   K–B1!

White's King is tied down to the defense of his King-side Pawns. Black's King, on the other hand, is free to wander to the Queen-side, where the decisive action will take place.

23 K–N2   B–B5!

White was hoping to free himself somewhat with K–N3 followed by P–B4.

24 B–N4   K–K1
25 R–B3   . . .

The exchange of Rooks gives Black a clear-cut win. But the alternative 25 P–Q5, K–Q2; 26 P–QR4, R–R7; 27 P–R5, B–B2 is just as bad for White, as Black gets a passed Pawn which must prove decisive.

25 . . .   RxR
26 BxR   K–Q2

The winning idea.

27 P–R3   . . .

White frees his King from the defense of this Pawn in order to rush his King to the other side; but it is too late.

27 . . .   K–B3
28 P–QR4   . . .

He cannot allow . . . K–N4–R5. But now Black finds a different way to penetrate.

(See Diagram 7)

28 . . .   P–QN4!

Here is the point where Black converts the Queen-side Pawn majority into an outside passed Pawn. If 29 PxPch, KxP and Black wins by advancing his passed Queen Rook Pawn.

The alternative is 29 P–R5, B–Q3; 30 K–B1, B–R6; 31 K–K2, P–N5; 32 B–Q2, K–N4 and Black wins without much trouble.

29 K–B1   PxP
30 K–K2   K–N4
31 K–Q3   P–R6

Position after 28 P–QR4
How does Black clearly establish the win?

Diagram 7

BLACK

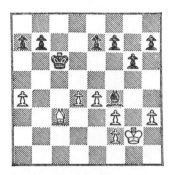

WHITE

If White plays his Bishop back and forth between Queen Rook 1 and Queen Bishop 3, Black immobilizes White's Pawns and then forces the exchange of Bishops and wins as follows: 32 B–R1, P–B3!; 33 B–B3, P–N4!; 34 B–R1, B–B8; 35 B–B3, B–N7; 36 BxB, PxB; 37 K–B2, K–B5; 38 P–Q5, P–KR4; 39 KxP, K–Q6; 40 K–N3, K–K7 and Black massacres the White Pawns.

32	K–B2	K–B5
33	B–R1	P–B3!

An important move. If White tries 34 P–Q5, Black wins with 34 . . . B–K4! Or if 34 B–B3, B–B8!; 35 P–Q5, B–N7!

(See Diagram 8)

34	P–K5	PxP
35	PxP	K–Q4
36	K–N3	BxP

Position after 33 . . . P–B3!
White is at a loss for moves

Diagram 8

BLACK

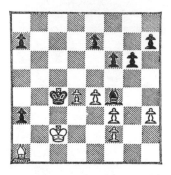

WHITE

37	BxB	KxB
		Resigns

Black wins the Bishop Pawns and proceeds to queen his King Pawn. A convincing triumph for Black's strategy.

GAME 2

(in which White's enterprising sacrifice of the exchange leads to a brilliant attack)

Match, 1950

WHITE	BLACK
Krylov	*Kozma*
1 P–Q4	N–KB3
2 P–QB4	P–KN3
3 N–QB3	P–Q4

4	PxP	NxP
5	P–K4	NxN
6	PxN	P–QB4!
7	B–QR4	. . .

A vast improvement on White's colorless 7 B–QN5ch in the previous game. The Bishop in destined to play an important role throughout the game.

7	. . .	B–N2
8	N–K2	. . .

And this is the other development which is essential if White is to build up an aggressive position.

Position after 8 N–K2
White is developing admirably

Diagram 9

BLACK

WHITE

8	. . .	Castles
9	Castles	PxP
10	PxP	. . .

Black has established the Queen-side majority of Pawns and

he is looking forward to a tranquil game in which he can turn this endgame advantage to account. White, on the other hand, seeks sharp middle-game play in which his powerful Pawn center and promising development will yield him attacking prospects.

10   . . .   N–B3
11   B–K3   B–N5

A somewhat artificial maneuver, instead of which Black can play 11 . . . N–R4; 12 B–K3, B–K3 directly.

12   P–B3   N–R4!?

This involves a speculative Pawn sacrifice: 13 BxPch, RxB; 14 PxB, RxRch; 15 KxR. The analysts hold that Black has enough compensation for his Pawn. In any event the extra Pawn, being doubled, is considered of no great value. This explains White's reply.

13   B–Q3   B–K3

Position after 13 . . . B–K3
How does White parry the positional threat?

Diagram 10

BLACK

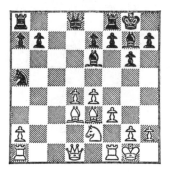

WHITE

The crisis. Black is on the point of playing . . . N–B5 or . . .
B–B5 with a fine game. 14 Q–R4 will not do, as Black replies 14
. . . P–QR3 with a view to . . . P–QN4. Rather than allow this
counterplay, White prefers to sacrifice the exchange.

14	P–Q5!?	BxR
15	QxB	. . .

The sacrifice of the exchange is based on a far-reaching plan.
True, White does not threaten PxB because of the reply . . .
QxB. But his Queen holds sway over the long diagonal; B–KR6
is an unpleasant threat; and Black's Knight is out of the game.
In addition there is the latent threat of White's advancing Pawn
phalanx. Black's game is in an uncomfortably critical state.

15	. . .	P–B3

To take the sting out of White's B–KR6.

16	N–Q4!	B–Q2
17	B–KR6	R–K1

White has the same reply after 17 . . . R–B2.

18	P–B4	P–K3

Trying to avoid suffocation, Black only succeeds in meeting
his opponent halfway. However, on 18 . . . P–K4 White has
19 PxP, PxP (or 19 . . . RxP; 20 N–B3, R–K1; 21 P–K5 with
decisive pressure); 20 N–B3, Q–K2; 21 NxP!, QxN; 22 R–B8ch!
winning the Black Queen.

19	P–B5!	. . .

(See Diagram 11)

A difficult move to meet, for after 19 . . . P–K4; 20 N–K6,
BxN; 21 BPxB White has a winning maneuver in Q–K1–R4.
Another possibility is 19 . . . NPxP; 20 Q–K1 (threatening
Q–N3ch; and mate the following move), K–R1; 21 B–Q2, P–N3;
22 QPxP, BxP; 23 B–B3! and White has a winning attack.

Position after 19 P–B5!
White's attack is becoming menacing

Diagram 11

BLACK

WHITE

19	. . .	KPxBP
20	PxP	P–KN4

This apparently shuts the lines of attack, but White finds new ways to open them.

| 21 | N–K6! | . . . |

This creates insoluble problems for Black. If he plays 21 . . . Q–N3ch his King Bishop Pawn goes, and with it the game. On the other hand, after 21 . . . BxN; 22 BPxB he is again defenseless.

| 21 | . . . | Q–K2 |
| 22 | BxP! | BxN |

If 22 . . . PxB; 23 P–B6, Q–B2; 24 NxP, QxQP; 24 P–B7ch, K–B1; 25 NxPch, K–K2; 26 Q–B6 mate.

| 23 | BxP | Q–B4ch |
| 24 | B–Q4 | QxP |

Black seems to be defending himself ingeniously, but what is really happening is that White is opening up menacing lines of attack for his Bishops.

25 PxB   RxP

Or 25 . . . QxP; 26 Q–B1! (threatens Q–N5ch), P–KR3;
27 Q–KB4 (threatens Q–N3ch), Q–K2; 28 QxP and wins.

Position after 24 . . . RxP
White wins brilliantly

Diagram 12

BLACK

WHITE

26 BxPch!   KxB
27 R–B7ch   . . .

This does not leave Black much choice, for if 27 . . . K–N1;
28 R–N7ch, K–B1; 29 Q–KB1ch, K–K1; 30 Q–B7ch and mate
follows.

Nor does 27 . . . K–N3 help. For then comes 28 R–N7ch,
K–B4; 29 Q–KB1ch and mate next move, or 28 . . . K–R4; 29
P–N4ch, K–R5; 30 B–B2ch, K–R6; 31 Q–KB1ch and mate
next move.

27 . . .   K–R3
28 B–K3ch!   RxB

Or 28 . . . K–R4; 29 P–N4ch with a mating attack.

29   Q–B6ch   Resigns

Black realizes that after 29 . . . K–R4 he will be mated in two more moves. An elegant finish to an efficiently engineered attack.

Some useful pointers

For White:

1. Be sure to play B–QB4 followed by N–K2 in the opening in order to obtain the most promising development for your forces.

2. Watch for favorable opportunities to advance your King Bishop Pawn and get your central Pawn mass in motion.

3. Avoid the colorless, simplifying B–QN5ch in the opening.

4. Avoid excessively defensive formations—such as protecting your Queen Pawn with B–QN2 instead of with B–K3.

For Black:

1. Make sure that your Bishop at King Knight 2 is functioning at his most effective level.

2. Play . . . P–QB4 at the first opportunity in order to engage White's center and to cut down the power of White's Pawn center.

3. Don't become obsessed with increasing the pressure on White's Queen Pawn to the point where you are blinded to White's attacking possibilities.

4. Generally speaking, simplifying exchanges react to your advantage as they enhance the likelihood that you can turn your Queen-side majority of Pawns to account.

Conclusions

In a psychological sense Black may be said to have the initiative. For without any effort on his part he comes out of the opening with two positional advantages: pressure on White's Queen Pawn and the possession of the Queen-side majority of Pawns.

The consequence: White cannot afford to sit back and await coming events; he *must* pursue an aggressive course.

However, this is not the whole story. If White is penalized for drifting, it is also true that rich harvests may result from an enterprising policy. And here there are two factors that favor White: he has a freer, more aggressive development and he has distinct attacking possibilities.

Above all, then, it seems that this variation is really a clash of two temperaments. An attacking player should do well with White and not so well with Black. A careful, solid player should do well with Black, not so well with White.

DUTCH DEFENSE

(Stonewall Variation)

WHITE	BLACK
1 P–Q4	P–KB4

Position after 1 . . . P–KB4
The basic position

Diagram 1

BLACK

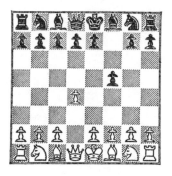

WHITE

This defense is imbued with aggressive spirit and for that reason has been favored by several notable masters of brilliant play, among them Morphy, Mieses, and Alekhine. However, as

we shall see, it is subject to some qualifications on the score of
faulty strategy.

Classical or hypermodern?

This query sums up the basic significance of the Dutch Defense. Instead of automatically answering 1 P–Q4 with the
classical–orthodox 1 . . . P–Q4, Black plays 1 . . . P–KB4.

The advance of Black's King Bishop Pawn is in accord with
the old theories of the center inasmuch as it is a *Pawn* move.
And yet its intent is hypermodern, since it aims at controlling
White's King 4 square from the flank.

This reminds us strongly of the underlying idea of the Sicilian
Defense (Lesson 2), in which Black answers 1 P–K4 with 1 . . .
P–QB4. There is a difference, however. In the Sicilian Defense
1 . . . P–QB4 involves purely strategical considerations. In the
Dutch Defense, however, the fact that the King Bishop Pawn

The Normal Pawn Skeleton
The Stonewall formation

Diagram 2

BLACK

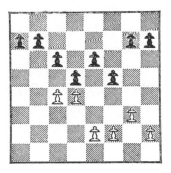

WHITE

is on the King-side has a special meaning. *Whichever player gets the advantage is likely to obtain a strong King-side attack as well.*

Since this defense mingles attacking possibilities with strategical drawbacks, it is a fighting line which has been favored by players who were well aware of its theoretical defects.

Strong and weak points

The origin of the term "stonewall" loses some of its mysterious quality when we study Diagram 2:

The combination of Black's Pawns on King Bishop 4 and Queen 4, supplemented by his Pawns on King 3 and Queen Bishop 3, is very sturdy and makes it difficult for White to break through without quite a bit of preparation. For this reason Black's Pawn setup is known as the "stonewall" formation.

The strong points of this policy are:

1. Black prevents White's P–K4 either permanently or for a long time to come.

2. Consequently, the position becomes barricaded, making it quite difficult for White to break through.

3. Black's King Knight often takes up a strong post at his King 5 square.

The weak points of this policy are:

1. Not having played P–KB4 himself, White is often in a position to drive out Black's King Knight (after . . . N–K5) by playing P–KB3 (after due preparation).

2. On the other hand Black, having played . . . P–KB4 *and* . . . P–Q4, can only drive out a White Knight which may have played to White's King 5 by capturing it with a piece. This generally results in a positional advantage for White.

3. This in turn directs our thoughts to another point. Black's King 4 square is a hole (see page 166); that is, a square in his territory that is no longer guarded by his own *Pawns*. Generally

speaking, almost all of Black's black squares are weak because his King Bishop Pawn, King Pawn, Queen Pawn and Queen Bishop Pawn are all on white squares and therefore do not command black squares.

3. These weaknesses are plugged up to some extent by Black's King Bishop. Consequently, the exchange of this Bishop may have serious repercussions for Black.

4. An accompanying weakness is that Black's Queen Bishop, traveling on white squares, has practically no mobility because it is hemmed in by the Black Pawns on white squares.

5. From the two previous points it is easy to see that White will always try to exchange off his Queen Bishop against Black's "good" Bishop (his King Bishop). The purpose of such an exchange is to weaken the black squares in Black's camp and also to leave Black with his "bad" Bishop (his Queen Bishop).

Summing up, we see that *strategically* the possibilities are decidedly in White's favor. But it is not easy to exploit such an advantage against a very good player. Consequently, Black should adopt this defense only if he is the better player.

An important finesse

In the discussion of White's Normal Formation the point will be made that it is more advantageous for him to post his King Knight at King Rook 3 than at King Bishop 3.

Black can avoid this advantageous placement by answering 1 P–Q4 with 1 . . . P–K3 (instead of 1 . . . P–KB4). Of course, if White is so inclined he can give the game a wholly different turn by playing 2 P–K4 (French Defense). Black has no real reason to fear this possibility.

Let us assume, however, that White wishes to play a Queen Pawn opening. In that case he is in something of a quandary. If he plays 2 N–KB3, Black replies 2 . . . P–KB4, having deflected White's King Knight from King Rook 3.

On the other hand, if White replies 2 P–QB4 he reserves the option of a later N–KR3—but he allows Black to exchange off his King Bishop by . . . B–N5ch.

The value of this exchange is not always clearly understood. Sometimes we can see a mistaken policy pursued in this respect even in master games. The following comments are intended to clear up the difficulty.

1. If Black intends to play a stonewall formation, he should *not* exchange off his King Bishop. For such an exchange would critically weaken Black's black squares. (Study the Normal Pawn Skeleton in Diagram 2.)

2. Suppose on the other hand that Black has already exchanged off his King Bishop. In that case he should avoid . . . P–Q4. The proper disposition of his Queen Pawn then would be . . . P–Q3, avoiding a weakening of his black squares.

3. But suppose White prevents the exchange of Black's King Bishop. (One way to do this is for White to castle before playing P–QB4.) In that event it seems foolish to play . . . P–Q3, as Black's King Bishop is locked in at King 2 and has no scope.

The proper course in that case seems . . . P–Q4 (stonewall), after which Black's King Bishop will be comparatively well placed at Queen 3. But, as we know, the stonewall formation has its drawbacks too. Our over-all conclusion, then, is that Black's best line—where White allows it—is for Black to exchange off his King Bishop with . . . B–N5ch and then play . . . P–Q3.

White's Normal Formation

White's *King Rook Pawn* remains at King Rook 2.

White's *King Knight Pawn* advances one square to allow the fianchetto of White's King Bishop.

White's *King Bishop Pawn* remains at King Bishop 2 for the

time being. Sometimes it advances to King Bishop 3 to drive off Black's Knight, which may have established itself on White's King 4 square. Another reason for playing P–KB3 would be to prepare for P–K4.

White's *King Pawn* remains at King 2 for the time being, but White's chief goal is to advance this Pawn to King 4 (as in the second Illustrative Game). Where this advance is possible, it is likely to smash Black's position.

White's *Queen Pawn* plays to Queen 4, where it has the important function of standing guard over the vital King 5 square.

White's *Queen Bishop Pawn* plays to Queen Bishop 4, preferably after castling in order to prevent Black from exchanging off his King Bishop. The advance of this Pawn has three main purposes:

1. The Pawn may remain at Queen Bishop 4 in order to keep the center in a state of tension and to prevent Black from freeing himself by . . . P–QB4 or . . . P–K4—either of which would result in some Black weakness, most likely an isolated Queen Pawn.

2. The Pawn may advance to Queen Bishop 5 as a prelude to a general Queen-side push with P–QN4–5, etc. However, this relieves the pressure on Black's center. P–QB5 is therefore questionable, as Black can react strongly with . . . P–K4. This should suffice for at least equality.

3. The Queen Bishop Pawn may capture Black's Queen Pawn, the latter retaking whenever possible with the King Pawn. Unless White can quickly follow up with P–K4, he should never carry out this exchange. Why?

The opening up of the game will be much in White's favor if he can get his pieces into action rapidly with P–K4. On the other hand, if P–K4 is not possible, then Black's development will have been greatly improved without any compensating advantage falling to White's lot. See the first Illustrative Game for a good example.

White's *Queen Knight Pawn* goes to Queen Knight 3 to prepare the development of his Queen Bishop at Queen Knight 2. In addition, this Pawn plays a useful role at Queen Knight 3 by defending White's Queen Bishop 4. In situations where White advances P–QB5 he will continue P–QN4, either to support his Queen Bishop Pawn or to push on with P–QN5.

White's *Queen Rook Pawn* generally remains at Queen Rook 2. However, in the event of P–QN4–5 White will often play P–QR4 as part of a Queen-side advance.

As for White's pieces:

White's *King Knight* should develop via King Rook 3 and King Bishop 4, as shown in the second Illustrative Game. Paradoxically, the development of White's King Knight to King Bishop 3 (almost always superior to N–KR3) is not White's very best in *this* opening.

Of course, after N–KB3 White's King Knight is very well posted, with strong centralizing tendencies at King 5. But the trouble with placing the Knight at King Bishop 3 is that it is difficult to play P–K4—an advance that requires a preliminary P–KB3.

White's *Queen Knight* almost always plays to Queen Bishop 3 to strengthen the pressure on Black's center. But QN–Q2 is an acceptable alternative for the following reasons:

1. To avoid blocking the diagonal of a fianchettoed White Queen Bishop.

2. To reach or control the King 5 square via King Bishop 3 when the other White Knight is at King Bishop 4. This possibility is hardly likely to occur unless White has played N–KR3–KB4 and missed his chance for P–KB3 followed by P–K4.

White's *King Bishop* plays to King Knight 2 (after P–KN3). It is the power of this Bishop on the long diagonal that Black attempts to neutralize by adopting the stonewall formation. But, as we shall see in the second Illustrative Game, White is frequently able to break through in the center. This makes White's fianchettoed King Bishop a standing menace to Black.

White's *Queen Bishop* plays either to Queen Knight 2 or King Bishop 4 (where the King Knight has played to King Bishop 3). In either case the watchword is centralized pressure on White's King 5 square.

White's *King Rook* should remain at King Bishop 1 (after castling) if White has chances of a King-side attack. In a purely positional game this Rook is probably better off at Queen 1. If White is angling for P–K4, either Rook can go to King 1.

White's *Queen Rook* likewise has varied possibilities. In a purely positional game the Rook may go to Queen Bishop 1. In the event of P–QB5 followed by P–QN4–5, this Rook is effective at Queen Knight 1, and in the event of P–K4 the Rook can move to King 1.

White's *Queen* is not easy to nail down. The best square for this powerful piece will become apparent from the trend of the game. The most favorable squares, however, seem to be Queen Bishop 2 or Queen 3. Here the Queen can support the vital thrust P–K4.

White's *King* goes to King Knight 1 in the course of castling.

Black's Normal Formation

Black's *King Rook Pawn* remains on its original square.

Black's *King Knight Pawn* generally remains unmoved, though there are cases of promising King-side attacking possibilities in which Black advances . . . P–KN4–5.

Black's *King Bishop Pawn* plays to King Bishop 4 in the opening and usually remains at this square. Here the Pawn has the important function of supporting Black's Knight after . . . N–K5 and in general exerting pressure on that center square. If White captures the intruding Knight, Black replies . . . KBPxN and thus gains an open King Bishop file.

Occasionally there is a possibility of effective counterattack by . . . P–KB5 to open the King Bishop. But this implies previous bad play by White. It also involves potential disadvantages in giving up Black's hold on his King 5 square.

Black's *King Pawn* plays to King 3 in the opening and generally remains there. Sometimes the opportunity for . . . P–K4 presents itself as a reaction to White's P–QB5.

Black's *Queen Pawn* plays to Queen 4 to close the diagonal of White's fianchettoed King Bishop and also to support Black's King Knight if it goes to Black's King 5 square. Black should never play . . . QPxQBP, as this collapses his stonewall formation.

Black's *Queen Bishop Pawn* goes to Queen Bishop 3 to support Black's Queen Pawn, thus rounding out the stonewall formation.

Black's *Queen Knight Pawn* generally remains at Queen Knight 2. Occasionally it may advance to Queen Knight 3 to permit the fianchetto development of the Black Queen Bishop. However, this will leave the diagonal shaky and create a weakness in the Queen Bishop file.

Black's *Queen Rook Pawn* likewise usually remains on its original square. In the event that White plays P–QB5 followed by P–QN4, Black may play . . . P–QR4 in an attempt to break up White's Pawn formation. Or else he may play . . . P–QR3 to hold off White's P–QN5 for a while.

As for Black's pieces:

Black's *King Knight* plays to King Bishop 3 where it controls Black's King 5 square—the great bone of contention in this opening. There are strong possibilities that sooner or later the Knight will go to Black's King 5, especially if White has a Knight at King Bishop 3, so that he cannot immediately drive away Black's intruding Knight.

Black's *Queen Knight* plays to Queen 2 to protect Black's most vulnerable point (his King 4 square).

Black's *King Bishop* is sometimes developed to King 2, but . . . B–Q3 is more customary because more aggressive. Consequently, Black's choice of . . . B–K2 or . . . B–Q3 tells us whether he seeks an active or passive policy.

Black should strive to avoid exchange of this valuable Bishop once he has decided on a stonewall formation; for after such an exchange, his black squares would be pitiably weak. It follows that if Black exchanges this Bishop through an early . . . B–N5ch he should shun the stonewall formation.

Black's *Queen Bishop* is the "black sheep" of Black's game. This piece has very few developing possibilities, and the ones that are available are none too favorable. As a result this Bishop is not developed until very late, to Queen 2. Sometimes it is played to Queen Knight 2, but in view of the stonewall formation of the Black Pawns it has very little scope here.

As we know, most of the Black Pawns are on white squares (see Diagram 2). This means that Black is very weak on the black squares; it also explains why Black's Queen Bishop has so little scope. Most of its potential squares are pre-empted by the Black Pawns. It follows that it is extremely disadvantageous to be left with this Bishop in an endgame. In fact, Black is almost certain to lose, as he is condemned to a passive policy.

Black's *King Rook* generally remains at King Bishop 1 after castling.

Black's *Queen Rook* comes into the game very late in the day because the development of his Queen Knight and Queen Bishop is so slow.

Another consequence of this slow development is that it usually takes a long time to establish communication between the Black Rooks. It is difficult to give any hard-and-fast rule for the placement of Black's Rooks. There is much leeway here, and the exact location will have to be determined by the course of the game.

Black's *Queen* has several developing possibilities:

1. Aggressive: . . . Q–K1–KR4. This generally heralds a King-side attack.

2. Defensive: . . . Q–QB2. Here the purpose is defense of Black's King 4 square.

3. Versatile: . . . Q–KB3. Probably the best of all. This move combines the attacking function of . . . Q–KR4 with the defensive function of . . . Q–QB2.

Black's *King* plays to King Knight 1 in the course of castling.

ILLUSTRATIVE GAMES

GAME 1

(shows how Black develops a powerful initiative against White's faulty play)

Pistyan, 1922

WHITE	BLACK
P. *Johner*	S. *Tarrasch*
1 P–Q4	P–K3
2 P–QB4	P–KB4
3 P–KN3	N–KB3
4 B–N2	P–Q4

(*See Diagram* 3)

5 N–KB3   . . .

The first inexactitude. 5 N–KR3 was stronger.

5 . . .   P–B3
6 Q–B2   . . .

This premature move is a waste of time. He should simply castle, 6 . . . PxP being effectively answered by 7 N–K5.

Position after 4 . . . P–Q4
How should White develop his King Knight?

Diagram 3

BLACK

WHITE

6	. . .	B–K2
7	Castles	Castles
8	P–N3	N–K5

Black loses no time posting his King Knight aggressively.

9	B–N2	N–Q2
10	N–K1	. . .

In order to drive away Black's advanced Knight with the thematic move P–B3. But Black has good counterplay.

10 . . .   B–N4!

White cannot very well reply 11 P–B3 because of 11 . . . B–K6ch. Perhaps White's best reply was the drawish 12 P–B4, B–B3; 13 N–KB3 with N–K5 to follow in due course.

11 Q–Q3   . . .

In order to prevent . . . B–K6ch in reply to P–B3. Nevertheless the second Queen move underlines the uselessness of the previous one.

Position after 11 Q–Q3
Black seizes the initiative

Diagram 4

BLACK

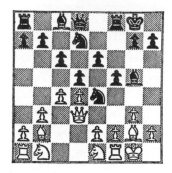

WHITE

11   . . .   Q–N3!

Very unusual, but the move has a definite point. If Black plays
12 P–B3? Black replies 12 . . . PxP! when 13 PxP is out of the
question, while 13 QxP allows 13 . . . B–K6ch and Black wins
at least the exchange.

12   PxP?   . . .

This parries Black's threat at the cost of freeing Black's game
White had better moves in 13 N–R3 or 13 K–R1, renewing hi
threat of P–B3.

12   . . .   KPxP

Now Black has the better game.

            13   N–B2   R–B2
            14   P–B3   N–Q3
            15   N–B3   . . .

But not 15 P–K4?, BPxP; 16 PxP, RxRch; 17 KxR, PxP; 18 BxP, NxB; 19 QxN, N–B3 and the position is overwhelmingly in Black's favor.

15 . . .   P–B5!

Virtually forcing the opening of the King Bishop file for Black's Rooks, as 16 P–KN4 would leave both White Bishops buried alive.

16 PxP   BxP

Position after 16 . . . BxP
At last White can play P–K4

Diagram 5

BLACK

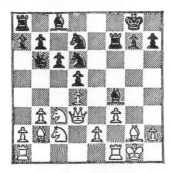

WHITE

White can now play P–K4, but the consequences would be unfavorable for him: 17 . . . PxP; 18 PxP, N–K4; 19 Q–K2, B–N5 or 18 NxP, NxN; 19 QxN, Q–B2, etc.

17 P–K3   B–R3
18 B–QR3   N–N4

Black provokes the following exchange, which gives his Queen access to the King-side.

$$
\begin{array}{lll}
19 & \text{NxN} & \text{PxN} \\
20 & \text{P-B4} & \ldots
\end{array}
$$

White worsens his position on the King file in the hope of stamping Black's Queen Pawn as a weakness. This hope proves futile.

$$
\begin{array}{lll}
20 & \ldots & \text{N-B3} \\
21 & \text{B-B5} & \text{Q-B3} \\
22 & \text{P-B5?} & \ldots
\end{array}
$$

This attempt to bottle up Black's Queen Bishop misfires. In fact, White's Bishop Pawn will soon turn out to be untenable.

$$
\begin{array}{lll}
22 & \ldots & \text{P-R4!}
\end{array}
$$

Threatens to trap White's wayward Queen Bishop with . . . P–N5 followed by . . . P–QN3.

$$
\begin{array}{lll}
23 & \text{B-QR3} & \text{N-K5!}
\end{array}
$$

With this powerful move Black wins the Bishop Pawn. It is all one now whether or not White removes the powerful Knight.

Position after 23 . . . N–K5!
Black has a won game

Diagram 6

BLACK

WHITE

24	BxN	PxB
25	Q–Q2	P–N5
26	P–Q5	Q–B3
27	B–D1	BxP
28	K–R1	QR–KB1!
	Resigns	

At first sight White's resignation seems abrupt. But careful examination shows that White's surrender is in order.

Black's main threat is . . . B–R6!! Even against 29 Q–N2 White can reply 29 . . . B–R6! winning the exchange (30 RxQ, BxQch; 31 KxB, RxR) with an easy victory for Black.

The most interesting play occurs after 29 N–Q4, B–R6!! Here are some possibilities:

1. 30 RxQ, RxR; 31 N–K2, R–B8ch; 32 N–N1, RxNch; 33 KxR, R–B8 mate.

2. 30 R–KN1, Q–R5; 31 B–N2, R–B7; 32 Q–K1, B–B8 and Black forces mate.

Final Position
Black's capitulation is thoroughly justified

Diagram 7

BLACK

WHITE

A beautiful game by Black, showing how Black can develop a powerful initiative when given the opportunity.

GAME 2

(in which White concentrates on smashing Black's center and exploiting his superior development and mobility)

Teplitz–Schoenau, 1922

WHITE	BLACK
E. Gruenfeld	*J. Mieses*
1 P–Q4	P–KB4
2 P–KN3	P–K3
3 B–N2	N–KB3
4 N–KR3	. . .

The correct development for this Knight.

4 . . .	P–Q4
5 Castles	B–Q3
6 P–QB4	. . .

Note how carefully White postponed this move in order to evade the possibility of . . . B–N5ch.

6 . . .	P–B3

Whether this stonewall formation can prove effective here seems doubtful, as White obviously has his sights set on an early P–K4.

7 N–B3	. . .

(*See Diagram 8*)

If Black plays 7 . . . PxP his stonewall formation is immediately shattered. White reacts energetically with 8 P–K4! opening up the game favorably for his pieces.

7 . . .	QN–Q2
8 Q–Q3	. . .

Position after 7 N–B3
Should Black play to win a Pawn?

Diagram 8

BLACK

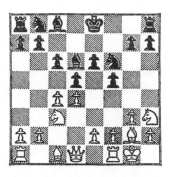

WHITE

Now that Black has resisted temptation, White guards his
Queen Bishop Pawn and prepares for P–K4.

        8 . . .   N–K5

To relieve the pressure on his game somewhat, Black prepares
an exchange before P–B3 vetoes the idea.

        9 P–B3   NxN
      10 PxN   B–K2

A preparation for . . . N–N3, which would lose a piece if
played at once.

      11 P–K4!   . . .

This advance is strategically decisive.

      11 . . .   N–N3

Black hopes to sink this Knight at Queen Bishop 5, but White
foils this plan neatly.

      12 BPxP   QBPxP
      13 PxBP   PxP
      14 R–K1   Castles

White threatened to win at once with B–QR3.

        15   N–B4   . . .

Black's best is now 15 . . . R–B3 (to stop N–K6); but after 16 B–Q2 he is in trouble, as he cannot complete his development and is meanwhile faced with a serious threat in White's contemplated doubling of his Rooks on the King file.

        15 . . .   B–Q3

Position after 15 . . . B–Q3
White has a neat tactical trick

Diagram 9

BLACK

WHITE

        16   NxP!   NxN

        17   Q–B4   . . .

Regaining the piece with advantage, for if 17 . . . B–B2; 18 P–B4 and the Knight is doomed.

        17 . . .   BxP

        18   PxB   K–R1

        19   B–QR3   . . .

Now 19 . . . R–B2? will not do because of 20 QxN! On the

other hand, if 19 . . . R–B3; 20 P–B4, N–N3; 21 Q–QB7! gives White a winning game.

19 ...   R–KN1
20 P–R4   ...

Now White's Bishops sweep the board, and Black is in no position to offer lasting resistance.

20 ...   N–N3
21 Q–KB7   R–N1
22 K–B2!   ...

White threatens 23 R–R1 with a view to 24 RxPch!, KxR; 25 Q–R5 mate.

22 ...   Q–B3
23 QxQ   PxQ

Black has survived the middle game, but he is headed for disaster just the same.

24 B–K7!   K–N2

On 24 . . . N–Q2 there follows 25 B–Q5!, R–N3 (if 25 . . . R–K1; 26 B–B7); 26 B–Q6, R–R1; 27 R–K8ch and wins.

25 B–Q6!   R–QR1
26 R–K7ch   K–N3
27 R–R1!   ...

Even stronger than 27 BxP.

27 ...   P–KR4

If 27 . . . R–N2; 28 R–K8 and Black is paralyzed.

28 B–B3   R–R1
29 B–B7!   ...

White prevents . . . B–Q2. Black is being reduced to utter helplessness.

29 ...   N–R5
30 B–R5   N–N7
31 B–Q5   ...

Threatening 32 B–B7ch with dire effect. Meanwhile it begins to look as if the Knight is heading up a blind alley.

31   . . .   R–B1
32   R–QB7   R–Q1

This proves fatal but Black is lost in any event, for example:
32 . . . QR–N1; 33 R–QN1; N–R5 (not 33 . . . N–Q6ch; 34
K–K3 and the Knight is trapped); 34 B–N4, R–Q1; 35 B–B7ch,
K–R3; 36 R–KR1 and Black is lost. Thus, if 36 . . . R–Q2; 37
B–B8ch, etc. or 36 . . . N–N3; 37 B–K7! etc.

Position after 32 . . . R–Q1
How does White force the win of a piece?

Diagram 10

BLACK

WHITE

33   B–B7ch   K–N2

If 33 . . . K–R3; 34 BxP and Black is helpless against the
threat of B–K8 mate. Any attempts at defense will cost him at least
a piece.

34   R–QN1!   R–Q2

Of 33 . . . N–R5; 34 B–N3 dis ch with the same result.

35   RxR   BxR
36   B–Q5   Resigns

For if 36 . . . N–R5; 37 RxP wins a piece. A model of first-class play by White.

Some useful pointers

For White:

1. Regard P–K4 as your most important strategical goal.

2. If possible, avoid an early P–QB4 to prevent Black from easing his game with . . . B–N5ch.

3. Don't be too concerned about immediately protecting your Queen Bishop Pawn after . . . P–Q4. An early . . . QPxQBP by Black may well lead to the collapse of his position.

4. Play for the occupation of the King 5 square while keeping in reserve the advance of your King Bishop Pawn so that you can drive away a Black Knight from your King 4 square.

For Black:

1. Concentrate on command and/or occupation of your King 5 square.

2. Having set up the stonewall formation, make sure to maintain it. Avoid . . . QPxQBP, which nullifies Black's whole purpose in playing this variation.

3. Try to be aggressive; passive play is fatal in this defense.

4. Don't forget about developing your Queen Bishop. Your Queen Rook is a prisoner until this Bishop moves out.

Conclusions

Theoretically this defense is inferior. Black creates several weaknesses which form welcome targets for White. And note that White is free from such organic weaknesses. Nevertheless, the Dutch Defense lends itself to aggressive action in the hands of an attacking player. The moral, then, seems to be that the Dutch Defense is a proper weapon only in the hands of a resourceful player.

Also by FRED REINFELD for Collier Books:

HOW TO IMPROVE YOUR CHESS (WITH AL HOROWITZ)